WHAT IS SCENOGRAPHY?

SCENOGRAPHY is becoming a universally used term in professional theatre practice and education, but what exactly is it?

This volume is a very personal and direct response to this question by one of the world's leading scenographers. The result is a provocative re-evaluation of the traditional role and methods of theatre design, pointing towards a more holistic approach to making theatre.

Pamela Howard examines scenography from the seven perspectives:

- Space
- Text
- Research
- Colour and composition
- Direction
- Performers
- Spectators

Part polemic and part critical analysis, the text is enriched with anecdotes and case studies taken from Pamela Howard's career and extensive research into the subject. Illustrated with brilliant examples of her own work, this book is a must for all visual theatre-makers.

Pamela Howard is a practising scenographer and theatre director. She is Professor of Scenography at Central Saint Martins College of Art and Design, London, and Visiting Professor in Scenography at Tel-Aviv University and the University of the Arts, Belgrade. She is a director and producer of the Anglo-Venezuelan theatre company Opera Transatlántica.

THEATRE CONCEPTS
Edited by John Russell Brown
Middlesex University

This series is designed to encourage a fuller understanding of significant aspects of theatre production, performance, and reception. Written by experienced practitioners in direct and accessible language, each volume introduces its subject and promotes debate about current practice.

Other volumes in the series:

Acting	John Harrop
Theatre Criticism	Irving Wardle
Architecture, Actor, and Audience	Iain Mackintosh

Pamela Howard
20 / 11 / 01

WHAT IS SCENOGRAPHY?

PAMELA HOWARD

LONDON AND NEW YORK

First published 2002 by Routledge
11 New Fetter Lane, London, EC4P 4EE

Simultaneously published in the USA and Canada by Routledge
29 West 35th Street, New York, NY 10001

Routledge is an imprint of the Taylor & Francis Group

Typeset in Adobe Garamond, Garamond Minuscule and Frutiger
Printed and bound in Great Britain by T J International Ltd, Padstow, Cornwall

British Library Cataloguing in Publication Data
A catalogue record for this book is available from the British Library

Library of Congress Cataloging in Publication Data
Howard, Pamela, 1939-
    What is scenography? / Pamela Howard.
        p. cm. – (Theatre production studies) (Theatre concepts)
    Includes bibliographical references and index.
        1. Theatres–Stage-setting and scenery. I. Title. II. Series. III. Series: Theatre concepts
PN2091.S8 H69 2001
792'.025–dc21
                                                          2001031765

ISBN 0–415–10085–2 (pbk)   ISBN 0–415–10084–4 (hbk)

"with what care he selects a chair,
and with what thought he places it!
And it all helps the playing . . ."

The Playwright's speech about the Theatre
of the Stage Designer Caspar Neher

THE MESSINGKAUF DIALOGUES

Bertolt Brecht
translated by John Willett

CONTENTS

LIST OF ILLUSTRATIONS

Cover illustration by Pamela Howard. Two small chairs made by Rajesh Westerberg.

Inside front cover: *Happy Days* by Samuel Beckett. Drawing by Pamela Howard.

Inside back cover: *Liberty is at the door: Blues, Whites and Reds* by Roger Planchon.

ACKNOWLEDGEMENTS

THIS BOOK IS DEDICATED to my uncle Henry Gatoff who let me watch him drawing when I was a child, and let me hold the T squares . . . but especially for all the European Scenography Centre MA Students at Central Saint Martins College of Art and Design from 1994–1998 who came on a journey of debates about scenography with me, and whose thoughts are embedded in these writings . . . and in particular for my colleague Edwin Erminy and our theatre company Opera Transatlántica and the Venezuelan performers of *Concierto Barroco* who, in Caracas in 1988, demonstrated how these theories can be put into practice, and how joyful it is . . . and for my friend and collaborator John McGrath whose book *A Good Night Out* is the inspiration behind so much of our work

and

special thanks to Fergus Moffat my agent and friend for all his support and to Michael Earley – the astute eye and ear. To Susan and John Harper – my listeners, to Mike Smith and to Stephen Unwin for all the debates

and

thanks to all those who have contributed to the World View acknowledging that without the continued existence of OISTAT, our world fraternity of scenographers (Organisation des Scenographes, Architèctes et Techniciens Théâtrales), the debt we all owe to Prague, the headquarters of the Prague Quadriennale and the leadership of Jaroslav Malina, we would not know each other.

And of course to Rebecca and Sophie with love.

This book is supported through a Leverhulme Emeritus Fellowship 1999 and by Central Saint Martins College of Art and Design London.

with many thanks

WHENEVER SCENOGRAPHERS meet internationally the discussion inevitably turns to that indefinable conundrum "What is Scenography?" Lively debates flourish that show the spectrum of views from all over the world and how difficult it is to quantify. Following is a selection of responses to the question that colleagues were asked to answer in as few words as possible, and the book is my own personal in-depth response.

What is scenography?

Jerôme Maeckelbergh Belgium	The adaptation of a given space for a theatrical happening.
José Carlos Serroni Brazil	The spatial translation of the scene.
Galin Stoev Bulgaria	Choosing a text to stage means to define your own world "here and now" and determine your priorities. But you never stay at one point, because your concept constantly experiences all kind of metamorphoses on the way.
Michael Levine Canada	The physical manifestation of the collaborative ideas.
Iago Pericot Catalonia	The visualisation of the dramatic text – seeing is believing!
Frederic Amat Catalonia	The evocation of a text or idea, transforming and resolving the scenic space.

xiii

Stavros Antonopoulos Cyprus	The visual intersection of the ordinary, with the imaginative.
Jaroslav Malina Czech Republic	The dramatical solution of space. If architecture is a huge three-dimensional sculpture in an outdoor situation, so then scenography for me is a sort of reversed sculpture inside (and sometimes outside) any concrete space.
Josef Svoboda Czech Republic	The interplay of space, time, movement and light on stage.
Tomas Zizske Czech Republic	A spelling mistake.
Ramzi Mustapha Egypt	Graphics to be seen by theatre spectators.
Vladimir Anŝon Estonia/Russia	This is the game of time, space and sense in the circumstances of situation.
Lilja Blumenfeld Estonia	The cross which theatre designers carry to the next century.
Maija Pekkanen Finland	The visible design for the stage: set, costume and lighting.
Guy-Claude François France	The art of creating THE playing space for all scenographic media.
Antoine Dervaux France	To make – and break – the performance space.
Achim Freyer Germany	To create an open and transparent vessel which makes wealth and character of the work experienceable and discoverable.
Dionysis Fotopoulos Greece	A self-contained design beyond the word – a meta-lingual image.
Ioanna Manoledáki Greece	The transformation of drama into a system of visual signs.
Erik Kouwenhoven Holland	The suggestion of space which transforms in the head of the spectator to anything possible.

Taurus Wah Hong Kong	Visual art and design in different media.
Tali Itzhaki Israel	Everything on stage that is experienced visually – in essence, a human being in a human space.
Roni Toren Israel	Shape colour and light turned into a non-real reality in a collective
Luciano Damiani Italy	Not one entity. It only comes to life when the dynamism of the human body penetrates the space.
Ezio Frigerio Italy	The work of an artist that cannot be expressed in words.
Kazue Haetano Japan	The life of a space and a vision of humanity.
Mitsuri Ishii Japan	The visual direction of the stage.
Ilmars Blumbergs Latvia	The art of space in action.
Hamzah Mohammed Tahir Malaysia	A visual art which includes dramatic, emotion and communication elements.
Dorita Hannah New Zealand	The dynamic role design plays upon the stage, orchestrating the visual and sensory environment of performance.
Pawel Dobrzycki Poland	The visual part of theatre performance created with all possible devices of Fine Arts.
Nic Ularu Romania	Transformation of spaces, objects and clothes into a universe on the stage.
Josef Ciller Slovakia	Materialisation of the imagination.
Meta Hočevar Slovenia	"Play Space".
In Suk Suh South Korea	The art of time and space.

Lee Byong-Boc South Korea	The creation of an actor in a non-verbal space.
Alan Nieh Taiwan	The quest for dramatic time and space.
Efter Tunç Turkey	Searching for visual images with the performer to create dramatic and plastic solutions for the space.
Richard Hudson UK	Choosing what the audience will see.
Ralph Koltai UK	What the actor has never seen – the director never envisaged!
Georgi Alexi-Meskhishvili USA	The world of imagination, the place where I can travel through the future and past and bring my own world to the stage.
Delbert Unruh USA	The complete metaphoric realisation of the visual world of the play.
Edwin Erminy Venezuela	The creation of a rich theatre out of little means.
Miodrag Tabacki Yugoslavia	The visual space of the performance conceived through an idea, shaped into a physical and architectural whole.

INTRODUCTION

IN A TINY OVERCROWDED house in the north of England at the start of the Second World War, a young man, too young to go into the army, is dreaming of becoming an architect. He has a drawing board in one corner of a room that serves as sitting, dining and working room for a large extended family. His collection of T-squares hang from the green painted picture rails around the room, creating a dark brown angular frieze. The room is always humming with the noise of people talking to each other in broken English with nobody quite understanding anyone else, accompanied by the unforgettable sound of tea being sucked through sugar lumps out of a saucer. Under the drawing table a small girl sits on a little woventop stool watching the scene, but having an important daily job to do as Holder of the T-Square for the young architect, my uncle Henry. At the end of the day's work, provided we had not been required to rush underground into a bomb shelter, I could stand on the stool and look at what he had drawn, and ask all the questions I wanted. At the edges of the paper he used to draw little houses, and little people seeming in a hurry walking across squares, pushing prams, or riding bicycles. Sometimes he drew crowds of people looking at something that had caught their attention, and all these people seemed to live in very big open spaces. I always wanted to know who they were, what they were doing and where they were going, and the story I was told was never enough.

I am often asked how I became a theatre designer, or scenographer, and how did I know that such a profession existed. From a young age I went on my own to see visiting ballet companies, finding the cheapest seat at the very edges of the upper circle. I very much enjoyed seeing the dancers smoking in the wings waiting to come on, or preparing themselves for the moment they would step into the acting area and become another person.

I realised that the picture they danced in front of on the stage had something to do with the story that was being told, and the moving colours of their costumes were part of that overall picture. I could see how the scenery was constructed, and sometimes I could see the stagehands moving pieces into place, and whispering to each other, as the dancers danced in another world of light and sound. I was fascinated by the on and the offstage world, co-existing, dependent on each other yet invisible to the public unless they cared to look beyond the ethereal dancers. I listened to conversations in the auditorium, and once heard an argument between two elegantly dressed men about the merits of the design we were watching. One man indignantly said of the designer, "He pays no attention to what the piece is about – he just does exactly what he wants, and it's the same thing every time." I thought this sounded an interesting way to live one's life. A short time later, in the class at school, we were asked to write down what we wanted to be when we left school. Most girls wrote "ice skater; ballet dancer; air hostess; hairdresser". I wrote "theatre designer", because I thought – I love reading and history, and theatre design just draws it; I also thought, mistakenly, that I could spend the rest of my life doing exactly what I wanted. We handed the papers in, and my future was decided. I did not realise this was only a questionnaire. I thought I had committed myself, and my job was now simply to follow the route and do it.

This naïve assessment of the job in fact is not so far from the truth. A theatre designer has to have an insatiable curiosity to find out about things, to know where they come from, and why. To look beyond the surface and discover the truth. The greatest gift is to be possessed by an inner eye of the imagination that can transform facts into fiction. Theatre design allows artists the pleasure of connecting drawing and painting with what they have read. Theatre design is not a lonely activity, in fact it is impossible to be a theatre designer on one's own – it has to be done with other people. Quickly the designer finds they have to have a good understanding of psychology, and be able to lead and motivate large teams of people from actors to old recalcitrant carpenters. A big moment of discovery is finding out that no matter how good the design, if you can't get it well executed in the workshops because of a lack of communication or clarity it will never look any good on the stage. It is essential to understand how to work with technicians, respectfully and positively in order to get them to scale the heights of your ambition. A designer has to be able to juggle budgets, assess priorities, know when and how to fight for more money or to agree to the inevitable cuts. Although the actors' salaries usually take the greatest part of the production budget, the scenographer is often seen by the public and critics alike as the last of the big spenders. Angry letters to newspapers will demand to know why public money should be spent on real leather boots, or pure silk costumes, or real metal walls. Although the argument may be tedious, all creators, including the scenographer, have to accept that they are publicly accountable, and they must know how to deal with these accusations. If the production has achieved a total integration of all its component parts it is unlikely that attention will be focused on one particular aspect. An artist, a diplomat, a financial strategist, and a politician seem almost more than enough, but a scenographer has to go even further.

Scenography – the creation of the stage space – does not exist as a self-contained art work. Even though the scenographer may have studied fine art and be by instinct a painter or a sculptor, scenography is much more than a background painting for the performers, as has often been used in dance. Scenography is always incomplete until the performer steps into the playing space and engages with the audience. Moreover, scenography is the joint statement of the director and the visual artist of their view of the play, opera or dance that is being presented to the audience as a united piece of work. Like any collaboration the end result is only ever as good as the working relationship, and like any other medium it is sometimes more successful than at other times. The scenographer has a responsibility to do all that is possible to achieve the best understanding of the delicate and complicated process of making a theatre work, involving the director, performers, other visual artists and the technical team. A good collaboration is not a reality unless the scenographer is prepared to go further than simply making a personal statement reflecting his or her artistic talent, exciting as that may be. To go further scenographically means to work seriously to observe the director's methods, the actors in rehearsal, the implications of the text, and to use this knowledge to unlock the visual power of the play.

Modern theatre design has moved forward from the décor and decoration of the post-war years, and with it the responsibilities of the theatre designer have changed. Nowadays, the designer can expect to be consulted from the beginning of production planning, and choices have to be made at an early stage. This means that the theatre designer has to start from the first point of training to be much better informed and knowledgeable about all the theatre arts that are part of creating an integrated theatre production, and to understand that scenography describes being part of that whole, and not, as design now implies, an applied decorative art. The scenographer has to work to achieve a seamless synthesis between all the component parts of a Good Night Out in the theatre.

Understanding scenography starts with understanding the potential of the empty performance space. It then considers the spoken word, text or music that transforms an empty space into an auditorium. From the demands of the text, the context for the production can be researched in order to select appropriate objects, forms or colours to be put together in a spatial composition bringing fresh life and vision to the text. A space is dead until the performers inhabit it and become the mobile element of the stage picture, telling the story which is enhanced by the use of that space. Space is shaped and altered by the actors as the performance evolves. The collaboration between theatre artists is then focused through the vision of the director, and this animates the empty space and fashions it exactly to meet the needs of the production. The final element to complete the circle are the spectators, who occupy the shared space of the theatre building and are the reason for the work to be created. Scenography quite simply considers all these seven aspects to have equal weight and importance in an integrated theatre production, each one springing from and being dependent upon the other.

I often draw at the edges and corners of the frame, creating places where action can unexpectedly happen, very like those architectural drawings with their crowds of people at the edges of the picture that so fascinated me as a child. I am attracted by the neglected, the incidental, the object that would seem to belong only to a scrapheap – the small detail that carries with it the stamp of personality and bygone use. These are powerful objects that on first glance may not seem to have anything to do with the subject, but have often become central to the scene. The personal eye of the scenographer is first and foremost that of an artist, but one who is not possessive of their own territory. If an artist chooses to work in the theatre, as a scenographer, there are multiple aspects to be encompassed. The scenographer has to be an artist who can understand how to work with and incorporate the ideas of the director, understand text as a writer, be sensitive to the needs of a performer exposed to an audience, and create imaginative and appropriate spaces for productions, like the architect creating his perspectives at the drawing board.

CHAPTER 1

SPACE Measure to Measure: Playing in the Space

Theatre takes place wherever there is a meeting point between actors and a potential audience. And it is in the measured space of that meeting and in the generation of that interaction where the scenographer sets his or her art. Space lies silent, empty and inert, waiting for release into the life of drama. In whatever size, shape and proportion, space has to be conquered, harnessed and changed by its *animateurs* before it becomes what Ming Cho Lee has called "an arena where the great issues – of values, of ethics, of courage, of integrity and of humanism are encountered and wrestled with."[1]

The world view of scenography reveals that space is the first and most important challenge for a scenographer. Space is part of the scenographic vocabulary. We talk about translating and adapting space; creating suggestive space and linking space with dramatic time. We think of space in action, how we can make it and break it, what we need to create the right space, and how it can be constructed with form and colour to enhance the human being and the text. Some play games with space, searching for its metaphor and meaning in the quest to define dramatic space. There is a complex alchemy between spaces and productions that provokes the creators to tame an unknown space into a space that eventually will fit the production like a glove.

Space is described by its dynamics – the geometry, and its characteristics – the atmosphere. Geometry is a way of measuring space and describing it so that someone else can visualise it. Understanding the dynamic of the

---

space means recognising through observing its geometry, where its power lies – in its height, length, width, depth or the horizontal and vertical diagonals. Every space has a line of power, reaching from the acting area to the spectator, that the scenographer has to reveal and explore. This line of power is actively felt by performers on the stage, as they look into the auditorium and assess where they feel most strongly placed. A production can be planned to exploit and capitalise on these strengths, so that the actors can be seen and heard to their best advantage. The characteristic of a space also has to be taken into consideration from the first moment of planning. Its atmosphere and quality deeply affect both audience and performers. A space is a living personality with a past, present and future. Brick, ironwork, concrete, wooden beams and structures, red seats and gilt and decorated balconies all give a building its individual characteristic.

Observed space has to be recorded, through accurate ground plans and elevations, photographs and on-site drawings, so that it can be recreated in the studio as a coloured and textured scale maquette. It should always include at least the first rows of seating, and have fixed points of view from all the extreme positions of the house. The empty maquette which exposes the bare bones of the space is so important because it is the first means of direct communication between director and scenographer as they start to work together. The lighting designer and the movement director can also see the possibilities of their contribution through the completed maquette. The creation of carefully made scale figures adds the human dynamic to the empty space (it helps if they do not fall over, and they often do), for the use and manipulation of scale on the stage is a scenographic art, that stretches space from the maximum to the minimum to give it meaning. These ideas can be tried out in the maquette and games can be played with the space by enlarging or reducing the size of a wall or door, or simply the furniture, or creating a deceptive space that alters the proportion of the human figure. Through this process the dynamic that the space provides can be moulded and sculpted until it starts to speak of the envisaged production.

Scenography and architecture are very closely linked, and many architects have brought their understanding of space to the theatre. Adolphe Appia (1862–1928) was the first stage architect of the twentieth century, and invented an architectural openness and freshness to his theatre spaces at a time when illusionistic painted scenery filling the stage was the standard arrangement. In 1911, in Hellerau in Germany, he created his Rhythmic Space – an arrangement of steps and platforms providing changeable modules of verticals and horizontals. Working on these different levels enabled actors to be isolated in specifically focused shafts of light, enhancing their presence on the stage in space without extra scenery, and began a quest for more sculptural scenic solutions. Architects are often visionaries and innovators, encompassing philosophy, art, music and politics, plus an understanding of materials and the ability to dream out loud. Erich Mendelsohn (1887–1953) was born in East Prussia, and buildings in Germany, England, America and Israel testify to his vivid imagination. From 1912 to 1914 he designed settings and costumes for pageants and festive processions, part of the German expressionist movement. He remade the interior of the Deutsches Theater, but considered he had made a wise career choice when he chose Architecture as his medium. His inspiration came from observing nature and landscapes while listening to music by Bach and dreaming about creating buildings that expressed the moment of the time, using all newly developed technology and materials. He drew free sketches from his imagination on concert programmes and scraps of paper and captured the spontaneous ideas of these quick and fluid sketches, transforming them through models into concrete buildings.[2] These soaring visions of buildings expressed hope and optimism in the dark days of world wars, and his own personal faith in the future. Like scenographers, Mendelsohn always started by being excited by the challenges and possibilities of responding to a space, describing his process as "seeing the site and taking possession of it".

His search to combine dynamics and function, and his profound love and inspiration from the harmonies and counterpoint mathematics of Bach's music, are evident in the early expressionist buildings. Using materials of the day, he created external structures that housed the working and corporate sectors within one dramatic volume. He created a spatial relationship between the performer/factory worker and the audience/client that had the same intensity as the integrated audiences and performers of the old baroque theatres of the early eighteenth century. These theatre buildings had internal wooden interiors, compact and organised. They conceived a whole oval space of stage and auditorium as one entity in which the performers played for the spectators that they could see and not at spectators that were sensed but not seen sitting in the dark.

The baroque theatres of Europe were largely constructed on an axis

2   Erich Mendelsohn, *Dynamics and Function*, Ostfildern-Ruit, Germany: Hatje Cantz, 1999.

leading from the centre of the performing area in a diagonal upwards to the centre of the Royal Box placed in the first circle of the horseshoe-shaped auditorium. A proscenium frame holding the front curtain marked the division of the space, but a forestage protruded into the audience, where allegorical characters could address the Royal box directly, in front of the curtain, and also be seen from all parts of the house. The orchestra, essential to all performances, was placed on the same level as the spectators. The spectacular event was the raising of the curtain, usually after a musical and spoken prologue. The stage space revealed elaborate totally symmetrical scenic arrangements of borders and flats painted in detailed perspectives that were perfect from the centre of the Royal box, and less and less perfect from the seats on either side. Once the curtain had been raised, the stage space was enhanced by candles and footlights, all focused towards the prime central position on the stage. The curtain was never lowered during these performances until the end. Elaborate scene changes and transformations took place in full view of the spectators, and were as much part of the performance as the masque or opera being performed. These transformations exploited to the maximum all the planes of the stage space, using the vertical height from above to indicate divine space, and the depth below the stage floor as the demonic space. Stage traps and winching devices could make performers and scenic effects rise from below and descend from on high, while each side of the stage held hidden spaces at least as wide as half of the visible stage, enabling perspectives of cities, landscapes, and buildings to slide on and off in parallel motion. Armies of unseen sceneshifters operated the heavy wooden machinery underneath, above, and in the side wings of the stage. Many were unemployed boatbuilders and naval workers from Venice and Genoa who brought their construction skills and techniques into the underworld of the baroque stages. Every inch of the theatre space was exploited to the maximum, and like warships, these theatres were working machines. Their legacy remains in the many technical words that connect boats with theatres such as "rigging", "splicing", "deck", "shackle", "winch", "pulley", etc.

There are many examples of baroque theatres still in existence in Sweden, France, Italy and the Czech Republic, with all the machinery still in working order. The beautiful Estates theatre in Prague, where Mozart's *Don Giovanni* was first performed, is typical. Exquisite, elegant and seductive, with a strong intimacy created by the raked stage thrusting performers into the oval auditorium, its original purpose was as much to be seen in as to see. In fact only one-third of the spectators can see the stage, and they have to be seated in the central body of the oval; two-thirds, seated in galleries and boxes that get less comfortable as they get higher, only get a sideways view of the stage. Mirrors on the sides of the boxes help to reflect what is happening on the stage, although the spectator has to turn away from the stage and towards the other spectators to see in them. The higher up the seat, the less is visible to the back of the stage. Any scenery placed beyond the halfway point of the stage is likely to be seen only by those sitting directly in front. In this elegant and beautifully proportioned theatre the seating of the spectators reflects exactly the tradition and class structure of the society it represented. The baroque theatre space continued well into the mid-nineteenth century, developing into the ornate gilt auditoria of the grand opera houses – built on similar principles, but much bigger to house the operas that had become part of national repertoires all over the world. By this time the enlarged orchestras had acquired conductors, housed in orchestra pits sunk between the audience and the performers. Although the architectural space had increased, the actual practical playing space on the stage was reduced as performers were obliged to sing arias as far down front as possible so they could both see the conductor and be heard. Composers wrote for large choruses that could make a musical and acoustic wall backing the singers. The symmetrical scenery of the baroque theatre gave way to illusionistic painted cloths that were only partially seen in the cavernous stage spaces when lit by limelight, gas and finally electricity.

The beginning of the twentieth century reveals a multiplicity of competing theatre ideals, then as now searching for the elusive definition of the ideal theatre space. As the grand opera houses continued to attract one section of the population, smaller and more intimate popular music halls created their own versions. One such is the Hoxton Music Hall, a small nineteenth-century theatre space in a dark part of London. It was formerly a local venue for popular singers, and fronts onto a busy run-down shopping street. It is a high, narrow, rectangular building with three galleries wrapped around a small stage at the far end of the rectangle, giving the effect of a version of an Elizabethan courtyard theatre or an eighteenth-century "corral" theatre. Although it has a faded and nostalgic charm, it has nothing to offer scenographically except itself. Assessing the dynamic of this space, and its line of power, it is the vertical height held between the galleries, and the small stage built on three levels with entrances at each level, that is the dimension to be exploited. Its character-istic is a long, narrow interior emphasised by a row of thin iron pillars with

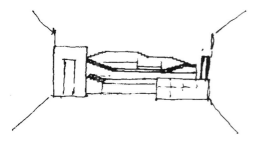

Figure 1.1   Appia's "Rythmic Space"

gold capitals on either side supporting ornate iron-work balconies painted red and gold that run the circumference of the space. Like many halls of its period it would have been constructed by local builders, probably by eye, for it is distinctly uneven and made out of rough, cheap, heavy wood that has now been painted dark grey. The three-level stage with small steps and balustrades leading from one level to another (Figure 1.2) is a scaled down, and perhaps unknowing version of Adolphe Appia's "Rhythmic Space" (Figure 1.1). When a production is created there that responds to the space, using actors and movement, simple furniture and props and imaginative staging, a real dialogue with the audience begins.

The intimacy of this space, inevitably emphasises the performer and the spatial placing of the action in the stage space. Space for the scenographer is about creating internal dramatic space as well as responding to the external architectural space. To be able to create potent stage images that describe the dramatic space starts with understanding and responding to the texts that are to be played. Throughout the twentieth century, starting with Strindberg's intimate theatre in 1906 there has been a continuing movement and search for spaces and forms to house chamber plays and smaller-scale plays that provide an alternative to the grand and expensive spectacle theatre. A neutral space, sometimes a black box, has developed as a self-contained dramatic space that can be used equally effectively in traditional proscenium theatres and more modern theatre buildings. If these neutral spaces have invisible technical facilities able to shape and reshape the internal volume of the space to suit the scene, a plain black box becomes a truly expressive space. The emphasis

Figure 1.2   Drawing of Hoxton Hall

is then focused on the dramatic space created between the performers and the object, and on the furniture or scenery needed to tell the story. The stage floor becomes the most important visual focus, especially if the auditorium is raised and the spectators are looking down onto the stage. When the stage floor is raked or angled to counterbalance the rising height of the auditorium, the actor's eye level meets the audience intimately, directly and powerfully, and a strong connection is immediately struck, just as one can feel when standing on the empty stages of the old baroque theatres.

By the middle of the century small multipurpose "*polyvalente*" studio spaces had become part of most theatre buildings. With shrinking arts budgets worldwide, these small studio theatres, conceived originally as a home for new plays, or cheap productions (unfortunately put into the same bracket), have now become the favourite places for making new and vibrant productions and are more popular than the main stages for both spectators and theatre-makers. There is a greater freedom to organise the space, and smaller budgets seem less of a handicap. Moreover, these buildings, direct and intimate, sometimes purpose-built and sometimes carved out of such unlikely places as the dome on the top of the Odéon in Paris, are always full. Actors like to play there, enjoying the direct contact with the spectators, and there are many scenographers who have been able to create and initiate original work in these spaces that could not be done on the main stages of the large houses.

At the same time the end of the century has seen an increasing awareness of the importance of conservation, restoration and recycling. This has led to a search to make theatre spaces out of old prisons, warehouses, soup kitchens, or factories. The change of use of the building is often deeply ironic. Former places of penitence have become places of pleasure, and dark industrial caverns long since bankrupt and redundant have been given a new life as temples of art. Instead of the stage being a fixed point, it can be placed in the most suitable part of the remade auditorium space to give the best possible relationship between performers and spectators.

In many cases, it is destruction through war or time that reveals the potential of a space. It is as though when the skin of a city is broken, its veins are revealed, and theatre-makers, always opportunists, leap in to fill the gap.

❖

In the port of old Jaffa in Israel, the former abandoned headquarters of the British mandate is falling to bits. Its concrete steps are crumbling, gaping holes are in the ceilings and walls and rudimentary electricity leads are looped crazily across the building. Into this unattractive setting, without romantic or picturesque seduction, audiences come every night. They enter a temporary building once prohibited, now desolate. But it has been cleaned and swept. There is a café and a bar, and the tables are simply upended wooden cable holders, and the stools are smaller versions. In a huge empty foyer space an exhibition of wooden sculptures painted the colour of concrete are illuminated by tiny halogen lamps strung on electric cables, each one perfectly placed in the space. This is no dump. The whole space has been carefully and simply prepared for the audience, and the aesthetic of the occupying company visibly declared to the audience before they even get to the improvised auditorium. In the performance space the external values of the company are reflected on a larger and more intense scale as it encompasses actors, direction and all the technical requirements of the production. The irony of this artistic occupation is not lost on the audience.

It is an exciting challenge for a scenographer to carve a magical space out of unpromising material, or to release a space by excavating and liberating closed or unused areas and making them habitable for both performers and spectators. Theatre is not simply a place you go *to* but a place you go *through*. Robert Wilson's installation/performance HK created on site in the old Victorian Clink prison in London shows how architecture can become the performance. The spectators or visitors moved through a series of expanding and contracting dynamic spaces that are themselves the narrative. The common ground between architecture, installation and performance is a growing interest of many contemporary architects who see interior and exterior spatial potential as part of the building brief.

Theatre is combustible, riotous and often dangerous. It needs to support itself with the right kind of space that will allow for the magic and transformation that best characterise theatrical events. Theatre finds a home in churches or on streets, in palaces and cafés, in attics or stadia, in exhibition halls, hospitals, drawing rooms and prisons, in a tent or the backroom of a pub. A designated theatre space allows an anonymous con-gregation to become a community, and provides a platform for their need to speak, to hear and to enjoy themselves. Cities are where audiences most naturally congregate, and dedicated theatre buildings – frequently the landmarks of city centres and urban pride – provide the formal spaces for these encounters.

Within a city are other spaces that are also a part of the cultural life of its people. Some spaces are public, in squares and streets, and others, less obvious, are used for sports, social and religious events that take place inside buildings. Alongside their public arenas, cities are also full of empty marginal spaces that sit unloved, forlorn and forgotten, where performances and events are just waiting to happen. Sometimes the city itself becomes a theatre, its surrounding buildings the scenery or the background for projections. Against its structures the collective memories and aspirations of its populace are played out in dramatic or celebratory ways. Space is a vital ingredient of scenography and dramaturgy – the ways in which dramatic experience is seen and given shape. With the addition of colour, image and words, space becomes charged with life and action, engaging through direct address and dialogue with an audience.

In front of the old Gothic cathedral in Barcelona is a public square. Here, at the end of the working day, groups of people, on their way home and unknown to each other, pass through the square. Many stop and form circles, put their plastic carrier bags in the middle and dance the slow defiant rhythm of the Sardana to the accompaniment of small groups of itinerant musicians. The public as performers, are silent. When the dance is finished, they pick up their bags and walk on. In another part of the square an old man dressed in a stained black suit and a beret makes his theatre space. He invites passers by to stop and see what he has hidden in a matchbox he keeps in his trouser pocket. He talks quickly and quietly without a pause, and as more and more people gather he pushes the circle wider and wider, creating a huge acting space for one performer. His walk is fast, and he moves so near the spectators he can see into their eyes. At last he has enough people, possibly 300, and the space is right. He walks around several times, making sure he has their attention, and then pulls a perfectly ordinary matchbox out of his pocket and shows it all round to the crowd. He is a consummate actor, for he only gives the story bit by bit. Inside this matchbox, he tells the silent audience, is a lion. He stops and waits for the effect. No one moves and no one denies its possibility. He opens the matchbox a tiny bit, and warns the ladies not to move or make a noise for fear the lion might get angry, jump out and attack them. He then tells the story of how the lion got into the matchbox, all the time opening it little by little. When he comes to the end, he suddenly closes the matchbox, puts it in his pocket, and without so much as a word disappears through the audience, who are left looking at each other in astonishment, and then laughing sheepishly wondering how it was that they could have   9 been taken in by something so ridiculous. Of course there is nothing original about creating an improvised storytelling circle of people in a public place – such events are found all over the world, from villages in Africa to busy commercial shopping malls. What was original was the performer's deliberate manipulation of scale versus space. He had discovered that the larger the circle he created, the greater the impact of the tiny matchbox was – and the even greater impact he could make by making believe a huge animal was imprisoned within it. This game of size and scale showed a masterly use and understanding of his space, with the simplest of means, that scenographers and directors dream to achieve.

Urban scenography – the occupation of formal and informal performing spaces – encourages spontaneous public gatherings and street theatre events. The building becomes the setting, and the performers act not only in front of the walls but often on them, defying gravity and safety and providing a human face to a concrete wall. This is a way in which instant history is created that will evermore mark crucial historic events and give focus to new aspirations. The connection is between the space and the participants, both performers and spectators, and provides valuable experience for scenographers who are always looking and searching for ways to animate space and use all the geometric possibilities.

In the centre of Belgrade four large boulevards converge onto the small Republic Square. Its focal point is the statue of Victory and the background is the pillared portico of the National Theatre, a stone edifice of square interlocking slabs reminiscent of something vaguely Greek and monumental. On the day I visited it in autumn 2000, at the moment of Yugoslavia's emancipation from the grips of Slobodan Milosovic, a small humble stage has been erected in the square with a few stage lamps and a rudimentary sound system. It stands empty, expectant and waits to be filled; a tiny space within a greater surround. There will be a mass political rally here to bestow public confidence on a tentative new government. The mood is tense and hopeful. Thousands upon thousands of people are flooding into the square and converging on this one spot, for without question this is where we all have to be. The crowds wait good humouredly, and nothing happens. For the moment the dramatic action is the act of being part of this enormous shoulder-locked audience, unable to move or see, but all touched with the expectation that a greater drama will soon be played out in front of them.

Suddenly, everyone looks upward towards the wall of the National Theatre. What we see is not some grand figure making an important appearance but an anonymous boy scaling the sheer face of the building in order to get a better view of the square below. Gingerly he places one foot on the thin bevelled edge between the stone slabs and levers himself up. Beyond his strained reach is the ledge of a first floor window. He dangerously swings his legs and nearly misses his footing. The crowd gasps and then falls silent. He tries again and this time manages to grip the ledge and hold on with one hand while he finds another foothold. The tension is unbearable and all eyes are on him. Slowly he hoists himself up and manages to turn himself round on the ledge. As he stands up to look down on the stage below, the crowd roars its approval. Realising his achievement, the boy takes off his jacket and waves it in the air like a victory flag. He has scaled the faceless wall, in defiance of safety and authority, found his footing and has triumphed. From the heights he is the conqueror of the space, and the people of Belgrade give their acclaim. He is the metaphor for a new Yugoslavia. It is a perfect piece of theatre.

Both the storyteller in Barcelona and the boy in Belgrade explored and felt the space with their feet, one creating a theatre in the round and the other leading the audience's eyes to the utmost extremities of the vertical space. This is exactly what a scenographer must do when first evaluating the possibilities that a new space may offer. Like an animal exploring new territory, the scenographer has to scent and feel the potential, and imagine what can be created from within the space itself. The first time in a space is a glorious private moment, providing the opportunity to walk round, survey the space from all angles and consider which are the commanding positions for performers in relation to the spectators. Edward Gordon Craig's dictum that "a designer should design with their feet as well as with their hands" emphasises the importance of walking and feeling the space, always looking to see how it can be moulded so that the actors are presented as clearly as if a human being has never been seen before. Sometimes the empty space can itself suggest a form for the production, particularly if the whole space is to be designed, including the seating arrangement for the spectators. It is a question of looking further than the obvious or immediate, bearing in mind the overall intention of the text and the production.

The Czech scenographer Josef Svoboda has defined his ideal space as a "neutral machine – a working tool, with enough technical facilities to be able to change the volume and shape of the space as the drama progresses". 11

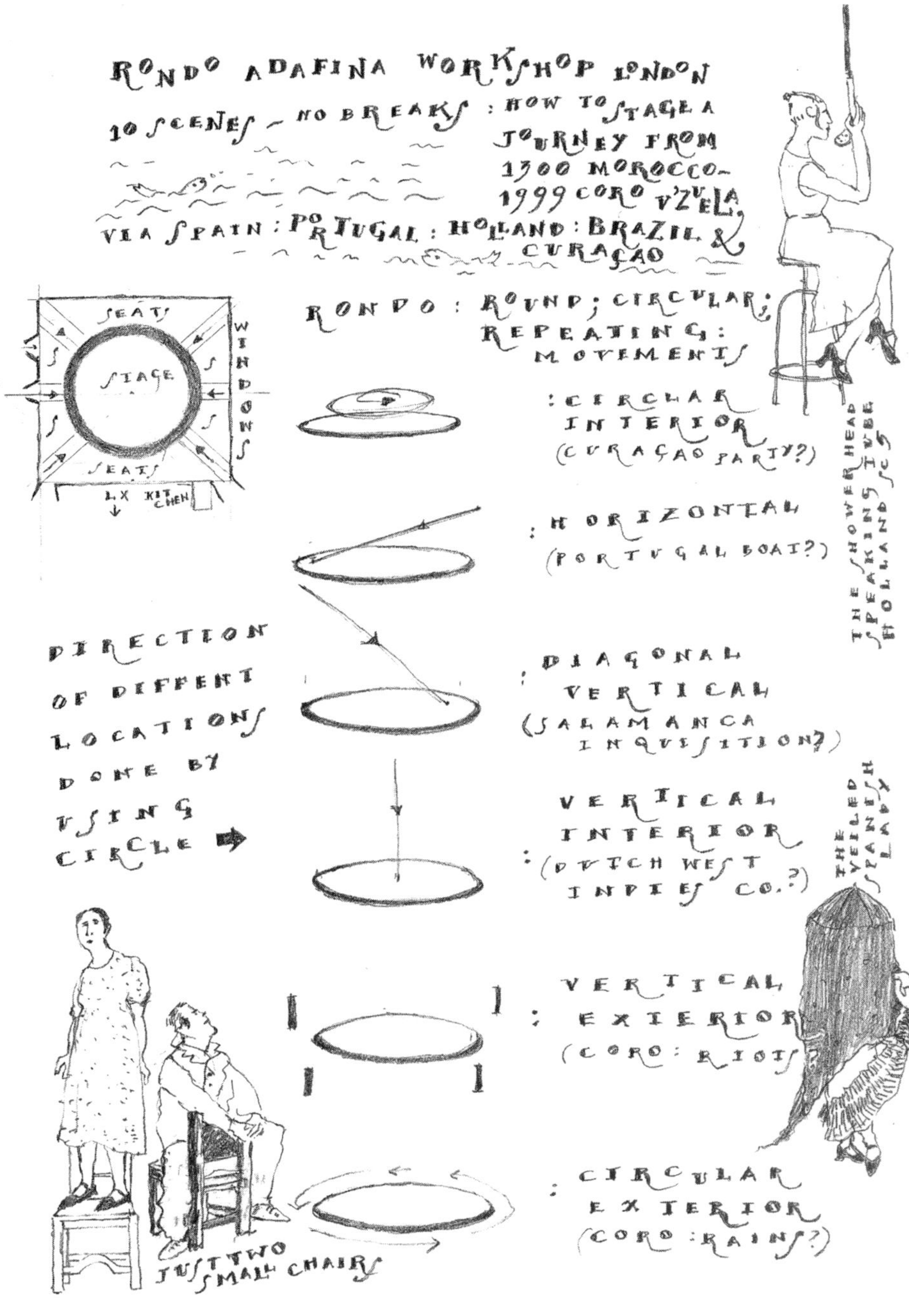

Figure 1.3 Sheet of small drawings for Rondo Adafina workshop

Many theatres have been built beautifully and stylishly as architectural showpieces, but are not working tools. Scenographers, the very people who use the space, are rarely consulted until the last cosmetic touches are being put to the finished structure, by which time it is too late to point out fundamental mistakes. The result leads to continual and repetitive expenditure as each production starts again from new. A "neutral machine" ideally enables the spectators to look down onto the stage, so that the stage floor becomes the canvas or background against which the actors are seen. The floor itself needs to be a machine, as in the former baroque theatres, full of secret traps and openings, masking an unseen basement technical area. Both the floor and the walls need to have working surfaces that can be painted, hammered upon or extended, concealing stage entrances and dressing rooms. If there can be windows with large shutters, or a loading bay that can be opened onto the street, this serves as a useful dramatic reminder of the thin degree of separation between real and dramatic life and time. Finally, a ceiling that holds the necessary lights, but is also a heaven, is needed to connect to the space below. In such practical working spaces, miracles and magic happen.

Such a "neutral space" was the venue for a group of transatlantic artists to create the scenography for a "journey play" (a play that moves swiftly through past, present and future, through countries and continents). We were working in a large, square, empty hall, discussing how to create a different shape for each scene as a way of indicating the change of location. We were looking at the clashing forms of Russian constructivist paintings and decided to translate this into space by creating circular "in the round" formats. By carefully judging the proportions of the two forms, the circle within the square created a dynamic tension and the visual and spatial language became part of the structure of the scenes (see Figure 1.3). This was an example of responding to the exterior architectural space, and creating an inner dramatic space between the placing of the figures and two small chairs that served to indicate all rooms and houses required.

The use of furniture or objects within a dramatic space and with actors is a vital part of scenography, and the way the stage space is described. The actor carves out space by his presence on the stage. Furniture contains and holds smaller specific space within a larger more abstract space. In the same way as ships are said to be wooden walls within a sea, furniture (especially sofas and beds) absorbs a metaphoric meaning from its presence and placing on the stage. These contained spaces allow the actors to use the

13

THE SOFA AS A ROOM — PRINCE HAL'S WORLD --

Figure 1.4a Sofa as a room

reality of the pieces imaginatively, and in so doing unlock their spaces, or entrap people in them, thus working in two spaces at the same time. A sofa becomes a room in itself when occupied by the teenage Prince Hal (Figure 1.4a), but a trap to ensnare an innocent rival when used by Hedda Gabler (Figure 1.4b). The actor gives the space a meaning, and the objects share the actor's space but create other internal spaces. A scenographer need never be dismayed by the author's furniture requirements in the scene descriptions (I always vowed I would never do plays that demanded chairs, doors and sofas), but rather can regard the reality of furniture as an exciting opportunity to create another kind of space. Just as an architectural space is assessed for its dynamics and characteristics, so is a piece of furniture. Scale and shape take on meaning, so that a curvilinear sofa set in an austere rectilinear room assumes a monumental importance, speaking silently of its history to the spectators. A sofa composed of loops and curves and vibrant colour set within a Sicilian woman's world of broken dreams and hearts becomes the very expression of the woman herself (Figure 1.4c).

THE SOFA AS A TRAP — AN ENCLOSED SPACE

ONCE HEDDA HAS LURED MRS A TO SIT THERE — SHE IS HER CAPTIVE ... DANGEROUS SPACE

Figure 1.4b Sofa as a trap

Edward Gordon Craig, in his erudite essay "Plays and Playwrights, Pictures and Painters in the Theatre" reviewing the many plays he designed, observed, "If I possessed a theatre of my own I should not convey on to paper the designs which are in my mind, but I should place them directly on the stage." However well prepared the work of the director and the scenographer is in theory while playing and developing ideas in the maquette, working with live humans in an actual space takes the preparatory work into another realm. It is here, in the actuality, that the performers' logic and reason unites the text with the space and the work

14

begins to take a real shape. The owner-ship of the space passes from the director and scenographer, movement director and lighting designer, to those actors who night after night will actually inhabit and use it, and make it their living space. Space is elastic, emotional and mobile, constantly changed by the performers themselves.

Figure 1.4c The Sicilian sofa

There are infinite scenographic possibilities with an empty space, be it in a traditional purpose-built theatre or a restored building coming to life again after a change of use. Each architectural space makes its own demands, but no space can attain its full potential without the action within it. A well-prepared production, beautiful to look at and beautifully played, can break through a prosce-

Figure 1.4d Sofa as a crib

nium arch and be as dynamic and exciting as any production in a site-specific space. On the other hand, performing a classic play in a new space, capitalising on the architectural possibilities the space offers the performers rather than filling it with scenery, can bring a whole new dimension in the production that often recaptures the interest of the spectators. Scenography is the actual realisa-tion of a three-dimensional image in which the architecture of the space is an integral part of that image. The image includes the placing and spacing of humans and objects, and this marries the truth of the words with the resonance of the other story that lies behind the text. The spatial image on stage is not purely decorative. It is a potent visual image that supplements the world of the play that the director creates with the actors in the space. To know how to release the space demands a profound understanding by the scenographer of the different disciplines of theatre-making, notably direction and performance. Planning the production demands a strategy – almost a guerrilla warfare – where the text and the space have to be infiltrated, captured and 15 questioned, and the consequences tested against the ethics and aesthetics of the creators. In Shakespeare's *King Henry IV Part II*, Lord Bardolph, in a war conference in York, uses the analogy of building a house as a strategy of war:

> *When we mean to build*
> *We first survey the plot, then draw the model;*
> *And when we see the figure of the house*
> *Then must we rate the cost of the erection –*
> *Which if we find it outweighs ability*
> *What do we then but draw anew?*

Scenography and space are here perfectly described.

CHAPTER 2

TEXT The Hidden Story

Language is completely central to theatre, and my commitment has always been to use scenography to enhance and reveal the text and the story behind it. If the disposition or layout of the stage space is eloquent and beautiful to look at, the audience can hear the play better. Presenting the subject matter, classic or modern, simply and truthfully, making it live and breathe, gives validity to the stage space and engages the audience. A spectator should leave the theatre moved and impressed by the quality of the play and not simply remember individual performances, stage or production effects, which are merely parts of the whole event.

There is an assumption that narrative and story-telling embedded in words is constraining and old fashioned, and there is a misunderstanding that plays that use words are synonymous with a theatre that has long since ceased to be relevant to contemporary life. Such an argument is erroneous and unnecessary. Playscripts, written scenarios, libretti, choreography and visual themes created by physical and performance artists all have a place on the stage and increasingly integrate with each other. Exploiting the physical power of the performer in the space can illuminate the text, especially if the performers feel confident that they are the primary story-tellers. Physical skills are as essential for performers in text-based theatre as in any other form. The experiments of Grotowski, Tadeusz Kantor and Jacques Lecoq did not deny text and speech; rather, they brought the notion of integrating text and vision into the exploitation of the physique of the performer.

Working from an existing text is my starting point and inspiration for finding the visual solution for the play. I think of myself as a visual detective looking for clues to pick up, that eventually, when I have them all, will give a surprising solution to the whole mystery of how to do the

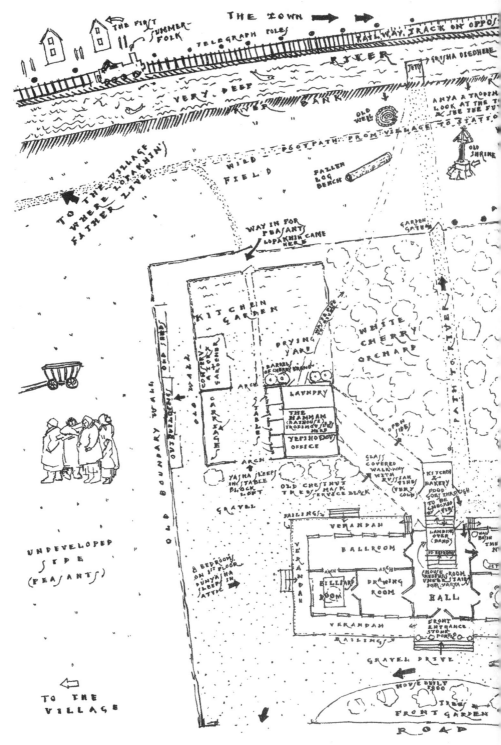

Figure 2.1 Imaginary map of the estate from the text of *The Cherry Orchard*

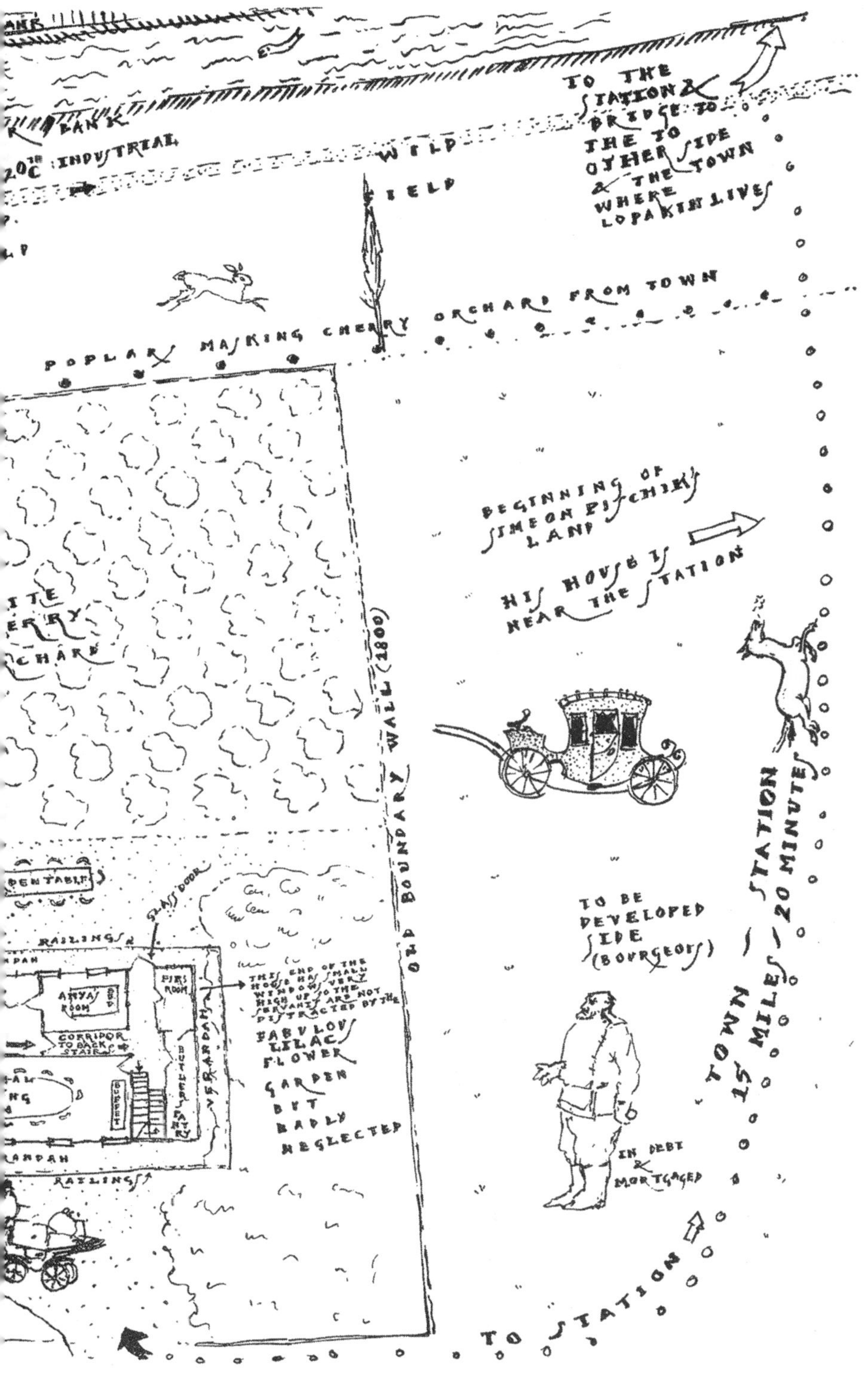

RIVER BANK

20TH INDUSTRIAL

WILD FIELD

TO THE STATION & BRIDGE TO THE TO OTHER SIDE & THE TOWN WHERE LOPAKIN LIVES

POPLARS MASKING CHERRY ORCHARD FROM TOWN

BEGINNING OF SIMEON PISCHIK'S LAND

HIS HOUSE IS NEAR THE STATION

SITE CHERRY ORCHARD

OLD BOUNDARY WALL (1800)

OPEN TABLE(S)

GRASS DOOR

RAILINGS

ANYA'S ROOM

PIR'S ROOM

CORRIDOR TO BACK STAIRS

VERANDAH

BUTLER'S PANTRY

THIS END OF THE HOUSE HAS SMALL WINDOWS VERY HIGH UP SO THE SERVANTS ARE NOT DISTRACTED BY THE FABULOUS LILAC FLOWER GARDEN BUT BADLY NEGLECTED

VERANDAH RAILINGS

TO BE DEVELOPED SIDE (BOURGEOIS)

IN DEBT & MORTGAGED

TOWN 15 MILES — STATION 20 MINUTES

TO STATION

play. More often than not, the text actually does give all the information one needs, but it is hard to trust it, and it is especially difficult to come to the work as an empty page and not to let preconceived ideas get in the way. The courageous way is to come to the text without having any ideas at all, allowing the words to sing and speak themselves into life. The text is unexplored territory that is yet to be mapped out. It is productive to read it many times, each time with a different objective in mind. First, isolating all the geographical references and creating an imaginary map of the landscape of the play visualises the writer's imagined world, even if that is not actually seen on the stage (Figure 2.1). From this map, actors can imagine where they have come from and where they are going to with a sense of logic and purpose. The first reading should simply introduce the story, and the characters who tell it. In these careful readings of the text, either classic or new plays, for proscenium theatres or open spaces, I especially listen out for the sound of the words, the "musicality" of the text, the timbre and texture of the speech, trying to decide for myself what makes this play different from any other – for example, the difference in sound between an Ibsen play and one by Beckett. This sense of sound is very near to the sense of colour, and later when I am composing the images it will lead me to a choice of colour keys in the major or the minor that visually mirror the music of the words. I am also listening to the urgency of the words and the material that is being spoken, and recognising the great difference between texts that are entirely spoken between the performers in their world created on the stage, and the text that speaks directly to the audience, as though telling them important news that has just happened and has to be conveyed.

Reading a play is never easy. The mind has an annoying habit of suddenly thinking about the weekly shopping or what to cook for dinner at night. People do not often sit down to read a good play like a novel. Some designers will say they need to do nothing more than skim the text, simply noting the change of locations in each scene, and leaving the rest to the director to sort out. In order to contribute to the production from a position of strength, the scenographer needs to be as familiar with the text as any of the actors and the director. A personal strategy that makes you the master of the text, turns what sometimes seems a daunting exercise into a joyful journey of discovery and an inspirational launching pad for the vision of the play. I find it very helpful to read the play out loud with a group of people, or just the director, playing a game with very strict rules. The rule is that no one must let anything they do not understand pass, no matter how long it takes to find the meaning. Everybody is permitted to interrupt and question the reader and ask, "What are you trying to say there?" After a few speeches (especially in reading Shakespeare), someone in the reading group should summarise in their own words what has happened, and the group must agree. From this breaking down of the text into small understandable units, the plot points that move the story on become visible and can be ordered into a list of "in which" – small sentences "in which a **person** does **something** to **someone** and an **action** results". More than the absolute minimum of words are not permitted and they must be active and accurate. This kind of intense reading creates the skeleton of the play that is going to be fleshed out and clothed. These "in whiches" become the titles for the first drawings of the images of the play that create a visual storyboard charting the action and development of the plot. It is absolutely necessary to include in the drawings the right number of people who appear in that scenic moment, for this gives the shape to the scene and indicates the space needed. These drawings are not to be thought of as "designs". At this moment they are no more than a sequence of notations drawn speedily and fluently, not intended as works of art but simply using drawing as a language of communication.

The next part of the process of transforming the text into a visual scenario is to create a chart of the overall shape of the whole play on a single sheet of paper. Start with a column down the left-hand side of the paper listing the names and brief details of all the characters, and then list scenes along the top with brief information, page numbers, time of day, locations, etc. Then create a grid to be filled in with extra information noting furniture, special props or effects. The aim is to be able to see from this chart the whole shape of the play. I love to make such charts look decorative as well as functional, and so where locations repeat themselves, as in Shakespeare, I colour code them. I then read through the play again, slowly and carefully, marking in the appropriate box the first appearance of every character in a scene, with a note if there is a costume change required. The final result is really a hand-drawn spread sheet. Of course it could be done quicker on a computer, but this is more than an efficient list, for when the hand records what the eye sees, it is indelibly committed to memory. On this sheet, reading across one can see the journey of each character through the scenes of the play, and reading down the columns one can see how many people are in each scene with the basic requirements of scenic elements, furniture and props. Reading across again, one can see where the possibilities of doubling parts occur, time between scenes for characters to exit and enter, and make costume changes.

Reading down again, one can see the size and shape of the scenes, and which scenes will need to be preset before the play begins. This chart also reveals where possible breaks and intervals can be placed, as for example in Shakespeare's *King Henry IV Part I*. The Boars Head scene (Act 2, Scene IV), is the largest and most complex scene in the first half of this play, requiring exits to other rooms, and places to hide. It has to appear swiftly after the small scene in Northumberland with Hotspur and Lady Percy, and its weight, texture and comic potential immediately suggest putting an interval break just after it. Putting together the numbers of characters in the scenes, and the requirements for staging, it is easy to see which are the key scenes in a play. These are not always the first and last ones. The chart shows where the technical problems are likely to occur, and from this information the production can be realistically budgeted based on the demands of the text and the staging requirements.

Plotting all the characters onto the chart gives another opportunity to study the text. From the "in which" list, the key plot points can now be allocated to the scenes, ready to be drawn in relationship to the playing space. First though, I have to get to know the characters in the play as intimately as my friends, for I am going to live with these people for at least several months. Every time I begin a new piece of work I have to buy a special new sketchbook or notebook that feels in harmony with the project, and this is very important. I go through the play yet again, this time following each individual through the action, writing down every-thing they say about themselves, and everything anyone else says or notices about them. I am building up a composite picture of each character as they see themselves and as others see them, noting indications of stature, physical appearance, class, and social standing. I then write a brief mono-logue as if I were that character writing my own diary, recording my view of my dramatic relationships and situations as they develop from scene to scene. I take information from the text that can lead me to imagine the character's life before the play begins, and what happens to them after-wards, picking up clues that are sometimes only given by casual remarks made by other players. It is the kind of work that actors normally do. This imaginary diary writing shows me the rise and fall of the characters throughout the play, and quite often it becomes clear that scenes hinge round a seemingly minor character in one scene, who becomes the focal point and pivot of a later scene. When I have done this, I have all the information I need to make a simple and clear character drawing that is the beginning of a costume design.

The final part of this text preparation is to go back to the "in whiches", always remembering that they are no more than a means to an end and not an end in themselves. Armed with all the knowledge recorded, I start to draw the images that relate to specific moments in the text. It is not necessary to fix the design of the scenes at this stage, for it is important to be free enough to introduce different ideas into each drawing in order to capture the truth and accuracy of the visual moment, and create a sceno-graphic script. Sometimes I have fun with colour, or like to experiment with different media in order to find the technique that seems just right for that play. I draw with a brush and paint, use collage, or inks. This whole process, which is free of the constraints of the production yet to come, should be utterly pleasurable and enjoyable, created in a spirit of enquiry. This is a time of total freedom where the imagination can roam, transcending logic and reason, making the most wonderful connections between word and vision. Using this careful preparation to know the text as one knows a love-letter also gives actors confidence to talk to you, and you to be able to talk with authority to all the collaborators in the team. Nevertheless during the rehearsal process it surprises me how much I have left out, or not understood, as the scenes evolve and more discoveries are made each day. This is the stage when the scenographer's creativity and vision are at their strongest. During this process the visual pattern of the play reveals itself and starts to be shaped until it feels right, looks right and, eventually, like cracking a code, will play right.

Towards the end of his life Pablo Picasso completed a series of small lithographs he had been constantly working on, based on the first Spanish classic play *La Celestina*, or *the tragi-comedy of Calisto and Melibea*, written in 1492 by Fernando de Rojas. It was first written to be read round a table over nine hours and was not translated into English until 1631. Until the first printed edition in Spanish in 1500 the author remained an enig-ma. His name was revealed hidden in an acrostic poem called the "Prologue", where the first letters of every line when read down the page spelt Fernando de Rojas. This great spoken novel is written in a cool, spare, elegant dramatic form. There is absolutely no description of location, and everything is divined from the dialogue and situations in which the characters find themselves. The "scenes" change in swift succession, and any staging that contemplates minutes of scene changing, even set to music, works against the seamless flow of the story. Because of its length, most productions opt for selecting passages that can only illustrate some aspects of this dense dramatic work. If the scenographer is an ever-vigilant detective, another story – the one behind the text – starts to emerge. The play poses more questions than it answers, and these unsolved matters hang heavy in the air as one by one the characters succumb to untimely deaths. The context in which this huge drama was written, apparently over a fevered period of two weeks, was the Spanish Inquisition with all its repressive laws, exclusions and censorship. *La Celestina* is a vivid portrait of the survival of a mixed Spanish society in the face of adversity. A society which had much to fear and much to hide. Scheming servants, dispossessed aristocrats, secretive merchants, prostitutes, Jews and Moors inhabit this huge canvas depicting a fragile existence where no one can be trusted. Each character depends on obtaining a few coins by exploiting his fellow citizens, and who can be blamed when the extreme divisions between rich and poor leave so many struggling like ants on an ant heap. The central character, La Celestina, is a soldier of fortune, exploiting opportunity to her advantage with practised cunning. Her language is full of allusion to

24   Figure 2.2   Drawing for *La Celestina*

her previous existences, for she is a master of disguise and can transform herself into whatever suits her purpose. She uses words of magic, devils, and mysterious religious practices, mixed with crude everyday speech, containing many references to the clothes she has acquired. The Spanish lover Calisto speaks courtly poetry in the medieval tradition, but his servants and the prostitutes speak in comparatively down-to-earth short sentences, not using any more words than they need to make their objective in the scene extremely clear. This economy of language, where gaps are left between sentences for the audience to fill in by implication, needs to be mirrored on stage. It is unneccessary to try to construct the town, or the individual houses the characters inhabit, but essential to leave spaces for these larger-than-life characters to command. The scenes usually indicate simultaneous happenings in two different places, inside and outside. The words must be trusted to give the location, and simple, fluid and spacious staging allows the audience to imagine rooms, streets, gardens and churches without any scene changes. To achieve this, the scenographer has to know the text intimately and be able to be a visual director, working "plastically" and sensitively with the actors to create small linked visual moments that will build the fast-moving world of ironic, bitter, black humour and tragedy (Figure 2.2).

The Irish playwright Sean O'Casey, over five hundred years later, was also a wry observer of human life. He is best known for *The Dublin Trilogy*, three much-performed plays depicting life in Dublin in the early part of the century. O'Casey's very individual observation of humanity makes the bizarre events of everyday life reality. "Walk anywhere, any day, keep your eyes and ears open, and you'll see fantasy everywhere you go." He sought through "laughter and tears" to put the world on a stage, and to do this by linking all the arts through drama. Dancing, music, song, painting pictures with people all form the architecture of his plays. Above all he wanted to combine Reason with Imagination on the stage. *Within the Gates*, written in 1933 and never fully performed, is set in a London park. The stage directions simply specify "sounds of birds", "formalised park benches" and "large formalised daffodils". The scene is described entirely in terms of its space and colour, and the time-span follows the seasons from spring, to summer to autumn. In the glory of summer, a "Chorus of Down and Outs" crosses the stage singing, a premonition of the forces of death. His other play, *Behind the Green Curtains* (not fully performed until 1995 in Derry, Northern Ireland), takes this interest even further, using visual and verbal metaphor in the text. Although there are detailed scenic descriptions, they refer to the symbolic green, white and yellow colours, and he suggests the stage should "take somewhat the look of a sketch . . . as if it is seen through an early morning or late evening mist". The green curtains of the title, that hide and divide, stand for the Irish hypocrisy and pretentiousness that O'Casey observes and benevolently attacks in the play. "Prying and probing. Ireland's full of squinting probers!", as the Senator Chatastray says, while hiding in an adjacent room with his colleagues to secretly overhear the pompous pronunciations of a visiting journalist (Figure 2.3). This sentence can be taken as the visual clue. To make this clear, and expose the humour, both the journalist in the room and the group listening outside behind the door had to be visible to the audience. Senator Chatastray's house, the largest in the town, was conveyed by contrasting tiny small-scale houses and trees all over the stage floor, against larger than life free-standing doors and windows set on a steeply raked floor. All the doors windows and furniture were truthfully realistic on stage, but the combination of different scales and strong colours reflected O'Casey's vision of life as a mixture of reality and fantasy.

Not all texts set out to be represented over generations. In site-specific work, productions aim to express a point of view, and speak more of situation than psychology. The very scale of the event dictates a presentational form of theatre painted verbally and visually in broad dramatic strokes. A writer creating a text for a specific space has to have a visual and spatial imagination to write effective scenes, and there is a logic in the

Figure 2.3   Detail from drawing for
Behind the Green Curtains

writer and the director being one and the same person. This gives the scenographer the rare opportunity to work directly at the point of creation and to use the architectural space to treat the play as a series of overlapping images that melt seamlessly one into another, conveying atmosphere and mood as well as location.

The writer and director John McGrath had been looking for some time for a suitable space in which to realise his epic history play depicting the warfare between England and Scotland from 1200 to the present day. He is unusual in that he always writes with a vision of the scene in his mind, and thinks in colour and image as well as speech and story. In the mid-1980s John had tried to get the Tramway, a Victorian tramshed, as his base, but had been refused. However, he had made Glasgow City Council realise they had an asset that could appeal to new audiences. In 1989 the city of Glasgow had been persuaded by Peter Brook to spend a minimum amount on restoring it for his company to present *The Mahabarata*. The building was made reasonably weatherproof, at least in the public areas, and a temporary licence was granted for public performance. *The Mahabarata* had attracted audiences from all over the United Kingdom. It seemed that *Border Warfare* had found its home, and John and I went to "first survey the plot". We saw the Tramway a few days after the Brook company had vacated it, and their seating block had been removed. It was eerily lit by mercury security lights at floor level, casting strange blue shadows onto the red brick walls. The detritus of a past event hung in the air. Empty water bottles, apple-cores and forgotten pullovers littered the floor. The extraordinary length of the space was ideal for the fast-moving scenes that John had already envisaged. We could also see the need for devices that would facilitate the action and lend themselves to short fluid moments moving from England to Scotland and vice versa.

John knew the story he wanted to tell, and had already done a great deal of the writing. We paced the Tramway space together and started to imagine how the moments and scenes might be realised. There would be a versatile set of musicians, and a company of twelve actors who would have to play over a hundred parts. Costumes suggesting the period and character, and which could be changed in a few seconds, would have to be devised. John had written the last act as an allegorical football match with Scotland at one end and England at the other. The two ends of the stadium would be united by a carpet of artificial grass with a single white line painted across the middle as on a football pitch. I thought that Scotland might be vertical and grey, constructed out of old packing cases

SKETCH FOR "BORDER WARFARE" BY JOHN McGRATH : OLD MUSEUM OF TRANSP

SCOTTISH END

KRIS'S LIGHTING TOWERS

6 IRON PILLARS

PART OF BUILDING

'KNOXMOBILE' A POWER MACHINE FOR JOHN KNOX & MRS THATCHER

BACK STAGE

TREES MOVE BEHIND HERE

Figure 2.4   Working sketch for *Border Warfare*
by John McGrath, 1989

28

RT. GLASGOW – 1988/9

)

FOR SCOTS.
PARLIAMENT
SCENE –

FOLLOW
SPOT

ENGLISH
END

CROMWELL
APPEARS
HERE.

BACKSTAGE

60

RED
BENCHES
HERE

BACKSTAGE

people
push
horses
inside
very fast
on wheels –

29

seemingly precariously piled one on top of the other to invoke a feeling of Edinburgh castle; England, by contrast, would be large, horizontal and made of heavy polished wood to give a feeling of authority and dominance. With this scenographic ammunition John continued to write swiftly and visually (see Figure 2.4). As the production took more shape, we evolved the idea of staging the play with different theatre configurations for each scene. One would be in the round, while the next would have a traverse shape, which would swiftly transform to an end stage by means of four rolling stages. The promenade audience would be flexible and moving and scenes written to make the most of the mobility and malleability of the space. Scenes in the Scottish parliament in 1707 were given an end stage format, as a theatre within a theatre, the few actors playing members of Parliament sitting in the audience who were meant to be fellow politicians. The continual journeys between Scotland and England took place on the four moving stages, simple trolleys on wheels pushed by stage management, or four huge carpenter's sawhorses mounted on wheels with realistic papier mâché horses' heads. The final act moved the audience to the full length of two sides of the theatre, revealing for the first time the metaphor of the football pitch. The large space became the signal for the text's invention. The need to keep the story moving through time meant that the text had to present events. It did not deal in depth with characters who were never in the scene long enough to be anything other than icons of their situation. *Border Warfare* conceived by a writer/director, achieved a synthesis of text and vision through scenography, lighting, music and movement that thrilled and excited the promenade audience who willingly stood for four hours every night.

Edward Bond has said that working with a new text carries a special responsibility for all those who work on its first creation, not the least because it is often unlikely that it will get a second performance. In the case of being the first interpreter of the text I have always thought that the text must be allowed to speak for itself with total clarity, so that what is remembered is the play and not a directorial or design concept. However, the writer should leave space for the scenographer to make an artistic contribution. If the scenographer can be in direct contact with the writer and invited to have some input into the dramatic structure of the text from the technical and aesthetic point of view, a scenographic dramaturgy emerges than supports the text from its inception.

This is precisely how the scenographer Caspar Neher worked with the dramatist Bertolt Brecht. Neher, though primarily a fine artist, was also a gifted writer and later directed a few plays. In the early 1920s collective and collaborative work was the order of the day. Neher was able to have considerable literary and artistic say in *The Threepenny Opera* and *The Rise and Fall of the City of Mahagonny*. He worked from the needs of the text, using the performers in the space to "paint pictures with people". The many quick small drawings Neher continually made were used as part of the evolution of the whole production, guiding Brecht and the actors. His personal style was simple, economical and elegant, but everything was chosen and selected with great care. This was not only to satisfy his own personal taste, but to be in tune with the quality of the text, the director and the actors, and above all the audience. Neher worked exclusively in traditional theatre spaces, exploring over and over again all the three-dimensional possibilities of the stage space. He detested being labelled as a *Bühnenbildner*, or set decorator, and was in retrospect the progenitor of what is now understood as scenography. Neher demonstrated that good work easily transcends the supposed barrier of the proscenium arch. The works of the great European directors Giorgio Strehler and scenographer Luciano Damiani, Peter Stein and Karl-Ernst Hermann, Roger Planchon and Ezio Frigerio, Ariane Mnouchkine and Guy-Claude François, and many others, have shown this. They have created scenes of breathtaking beauty and audacity that have immediately thrown a new light on well-loved texts and introduced new writing.

Roger Planchon's own original history play about the French Revolution, *Blues, Whites and Reds*, was first written and directed by him, designed by André Acquart at his theatre, the Théâtre Nationale Populaire in Villeurbanne, France, in 1967, and revised in 1971. In 1974 it was directed in England by John Burgess (also its translator) and Michael Simpson with my designs. It had the distinction of being the only play of Planchon's to be produced abroad by another company. The text is written in a formal story-telling style that ellides the misfortunes of a bourgeois family, the "blues" with a group of aristocrats the "whites". Their story is interrupted with short declamatory statements and songs from the dead men of Paris, the ghosts of the "reds" or common people, evoking, as in the popular prints of 1789, events of the French Revolution familiar to a modern audience as their history, but also seemingly removed from the present. The narrative story is set in provincial France, far away in time and distance from the revolutionary events happening in Paris. Everyone's lives are nevertheless profoundly affected. Planchon invented a highly individual and original form of speech that distinguished the three themes. The production had to be able to move easily between these different worlds. The text was seductively easy to read, but as the investigation probed beneath the surface it was found to contain a complex web of ideas, all of which had to be given equal value in the staging. Many phrases, particularly in the sung texts of the popular prints, contained invented words, or odd juxtapositions of lines, sung to adaptations of *carmagnoles* or popular French folk tunes in sorrowful hoarse voices. Famous personalities of the French Revolution are portrayed naïvely, as in street demonstrations, by huge effigies.

These giant effigies had to be made out of materials that would echo the ghostliness and sadness that the quality of the writing conveyed. The sans-culottes were ordinary people whose lives were not in their control. The effigies showed their hopes and ideals. We had to work very hard to make the spectators believe that the effigies had been made by the dead people themselves, and not by a scenographer. In the original French production the American Bread and Puppet theatre had created these images, using their favourite sticks, sheets and string. The idea was that they had been constructed from discarded everyday items that had once belonged to the sans-culottes but could also have belonged to a contemporary audience. Planchon's writing of the narrative story, that alternates with the popular prints, uses a contrasting brittle, sharp, and elegant form of speech. The characters talk to each other, rather than confronting the spectators as the sans-culottes do. The text conveyed a delicate balance between these two opposites, the real world and the underworld. The scene changes were as much verbal, as visual and a scenographic translation of the text had to be created. The brittle sharp images in the narrative scenes had to be in extreme contrast to the hoarse whispered quality of the Dead Men of Paris. The sound of the words was expressed visually through colour using a strong and heightened palette quoted from genre paintings of David, Greuze, Chardin and Delacroix. The costumes for the narrative scenes were made from antique silks, ribbons and brocades found in markets. By contrast the faded reds, whites, and blues of the sans-culottes' clothing were made from thin muslin and calico, the three colours dyed in and then bleached out to give just the faintest vestige of colour. The shared space of the stage floor represented ancient incised gravestones and was laid across the wide front of the stage, reminiscent of the surface of a Roman square in France. The back two-thirds of the stage were removed and a large full-width staircase was installed descending to the basement of the theatre.

A huge double gauze backcloth like a bleached-out tricolor was hung, opening to a V-shape at the top to let light in between the two layers. The blood-red horizontal stripe of the flag descended the full depth to the basement and represented the grave that the Dead Men of Paris would rise up from. Between the stairs and the concrete floor was a low wooden wall which rose and fell between each narrative scene with a sickening thud, like the action of a guillotine. Each scene was announced by actors running on and unfurling a banner showing the title and location of the action. There was a mechanical movement to the scenes that corresponded to the change of mood of the text. The dead sans-culottes surged up from their basement grave onto the stage to tell the audience through song and grotesque puppet imagery the urgent news of the day – "Ladies and Gentlemen, Liberty is at the Door!" She then turns sadly to the audience and produces an old torn sheet from her pocket on which the question is daubed: "Where now?" She lets it drop to the floor. I worked directly on stage with the actors and the effigies to discover their potential, and how they would move to the music. We invented musical instruments and sounds out of the materials we found to hand. Our point of reference was always "What is the text saying at this point?" We had to be extremely rigorous, judging whether we were really telling the story or in danger of being seduced by our own ingenuity.

The scenographer visually liberates the text and the story behind it, by creating a world in which the eyes see what the ears do not hear. Resonances of the text are visualised through fragments and memories that reverberate in the spectators subconscious, suggesting rather than illustrating the words. Plays transcend geographic boundaries, and are appreciated and understood in their original language as well as in translation, and belong not to nations but to audiences. The scenographer has an immense responsibility to bring a fresh vision and life to a text, so that drama is enjoyed as a living contemporary art and not as a museum exhibit.

CHAPTER 3

RESEARCH: Asking Question – Finding Answers

A scenographer is by nature a cultural magpie, delighting in the search for the ephemera of history and sociology. The variety of work that presents itself is part of the fascination of the subject, and satisfies an inherent and insatiable curiosity that wants to know not only the great events of history but the precise details of how people lived, ate, dressed, washed, and earned their livelihood. The challenge for the scenographic researcher is to know how to use an individual eye to ferret out the essence of the subject, hunt it down, and then decide whether or not to use it.

Historical research opens windows onto the world of the play that may not be described in the text, but which nevertheless motivates and affects the characters' behaviour. Parallel discoveries in arts, science, industry and commerce show how interconnected the world is. Few events are isolated incidents, and as the links between countries and people get more and more intertwined, research reveals more similarities than differences. Although historic events are coloured by national perspectives particular to their time and place, the very ordinariness and repetition of people's daily lives through the centuries is also history and connects immediately with the present-day spectator. The visual artist deals in extracting the essence from actuality, and presenting it with clarity on the canvas. The viewer's memory and recognition is activated, seeing through the selective eye of the artist, clothing, objects, or colours, that reawaken forgotten memories and provoke the joy of recognition. The spectator is connected to the subject when a scenographer has been able to choose an object which expresses more than its physical reality. A classic example is the hat that Winnie wears in Samuel Beckett's *Happy Days*, where only her head is seen; 35

from this hat the audience has to be able to imagine her previous life as she says "in the old style".

Creative research demands a double-pronged attack on the subject. On the one hand exploring the amorphous large picture, encompassing contemporary historic events, allows the imagination to roam freely in large sweeps across continents and history. On the other hand research has to be focused on specific, even tiny, details that can be taken from the clues embodied in the text. Scenographic storytelling brings an individual angle to a well-known work, so that it can be presented freshly to the audience. Researching is detective work – a hunt for the visual clues embedded in the text. The ground has to be carefully prepared. In practice this means slow and deliberate reading of the text, and interrogating it with questions to be answered.

Writers often have a very clear idea of the feeling and atmosphere necessary for the play, but either over-describe it, or do not describe it at all. For example, in Henrik Ibsen's *Hedda Gabler*, written in 1890, the scene is described as taking place in Tesman's villa on the west side of town – "a large drawing-room, well furnished, in good taste and decorated in dark colours, etc." It is soon discovered that it is not Tesman's or Hedda's decoration since the house has been acquired for them while they were away. Clue 1: They are living in someone else's decorations. It is then revealed that the house is too expensive for them and so large that they have extra rooms, and Tesman says he could not "ask Hedda to live in some little suburban house". Why are they living there? The house and its furniture have to give the impression that Tesman and Hedda are living way beyond their means. At the end of Act One, Tesman, in a clumsy attempt to come close to Hedda, says "Think Hedda, it's the home we both used to dream of – that we fell in love with." So is the story that they saw this house and Hedda fell in love with it and wanted it? Is the house "modern" compared to the bourgeois norm of 1898? Then the next clue is given in Act Two when Hedda describes to Judge Brack how she felt sorry for Tesman in the previous summer and allowed him to escort her home; "and so to help him out, I just said quite casually – that I should like to live here in this villa". A few lines later it is revealed that the villa belonged to the late Mrs Falk, and although it has been got ready in their absence for the young couple, it still carries the "smell of lavender and dried roses in all the rooms". The late Mrs Falk was probably elderly and the house obviously has been empty; it is not a modernist building of the turn of the century, but more likely embodies all the values of Norwegian affluence.

This example demonstrates how clues hidden in the text can be exposed, and used to build the picture of the play and the story behind it.

Creative research is much more than photocopying black and white pictures out of books, although museum libraries, bookshops, galleries, and the Internet are good and obvious starting points. Research sharpens the senses to see and recognise when something can be useful and appropriate. The painter and socialist John Ruskin said, "there is nothing like drawing for teaching us to see". A reference found in a book, and committed to memory by an urgent, serious and energetic drawing, is lodged in the memory bank forever. Artists have recorded the details of daily life throughout history through observed drawings, which remain forever as primary research sources. The objective of visual research is to be able to inform not only the vision of the play but also to pass on this information, to support the actors and the director in their researches during the rehearsal period.

Paintings demonstrate that all art is the product and reflection of its age, and irrespective of its narrative or subject is rich with incidental detail that opens a window on its world. Visiting galleries and collecting postcard reproductions, filing them for easy reference, builds the most valuable scenographic resource – a visual reference library. Painters, sculptors, and graphic artists clearly reflect the taste, mood, and atmosphere of their moment, and they leave for future generations encyclopaedias of information, and abundant special details. Jacques-Louis David, the pre-eminent painter of the French Revolution, mirrored in his paintings the changing face of France as it moved from Royalism to Revolution. David's early neo-classic paintings of grandiose subjects, through to the later popular prints and his designs for the revolutionary "grand fêtes" – the popular theatrical manifestations of a nation's aspirations – reveal the life lived by the extremes of French society. That can then be complemented by looking at the paintings of Greuze or the popular tin cut-outs and engravings of the Lesueur brothers in the Musée Carnavalet in Paris. One day I retraced the steps of a sans-culotte en route to storming the Bastille, from a copy I was loaned of a period hand-scribbled map found in the museum archive. I walked through the turning twisty lanes of the ancient Marais, imagining how the revolutionaries could have hidden and re-grouped themselves. Little wonder that later Paris was laid out in long straight avenues with clear vistas from one end to the other for easy crowd control. Visual research also reveals the most important icon – the scale of the ordinary mortal to the architecture. There is a great difference for example between the prominent human forms in the paintings of Piero della Francesca, set against smaller architecture, compared to the small human beings dominated by great monuments depicted by the Russian realist painters of the 1930s. Capturing this sense of proportion and translating it scenographically is one way of describing a whole historic period on the stage. Prints, ceramics, textile decorations, and other ephemera contain a wealth of visual information ready to be recycled rather than reproduced into the world of the play that is being recreated.

Sharing the research discoveries with everyone involved in the production, so that it can feed into the work is vital. One way to do this is to transform the empty walls of the rehearsal room into a vibrant "Living Museum" where the pictorial research information can be absorbed almost by osmosis and act as a point of reference for performers, directors, and production staff. Quick and free drawings taped to the walls, collections of coloured objects, perhaps relating to the emotional life of a character, old photographs grouped together, samples of textiles, pictures of chairs, printed ephemera, historical or imaginary maps of the world of the play, all help the performance. It also puts visual art firmly on the daily agenda, for the presence of the scenographer is never "out of sight, out of mind", and the actors can be encouraged to add to this Living Museum. In research, there is not only an academic rigour but also a naïve childish pleasure at the joy of discovery and at connections made between seemingly disparate objects. Every scenographer knows that the obligatory presentation of the model, and sometimes costume drawings on the first day of rehearsals, is politely received by actors, whose main concern is how they will find a way to surmount the immediate problems they foresee. How soon the presentation is forgotten, as the stage management mark out the set in tape on the floor, and the director and actors start to work on the scenes moving happily through walls that they have just seen in the model, but three hours later cannot remember on the rehearsal room floor. When the presentation is incorporated into the Living Museum, and the designs are left there, the actors are invited to enter into the world that has been created; the research thus becomes an organic component of the whole production. This requires duplicating drawings and sketches of the model to stay in the rehearsal room while the model goes to the scene construction shop, and copying original costume designs before sending them to the makers so they can remain in the actors' minds. If they are obvious on the walls, a gay and colourful gallery is created and the vision remains the crucible of the work and not an external appendage – a constant reminder of the visual reality that will soon be presented to an audience. The actors can be encouraged to put copies of the costume drawings in their dressing rooms, with samples of possible materials, so they can work with the feel and texture of the fabrics in mind. The budget should allow the furniture to be in rehearsals from the beginning, so that, supported by the research, the actors can begin to "own" the objects that they have to work with. Integrating the ongoing research work into the process puts a responsibility onto the production company to provide a dedicated space, with privacy, an atelier, near to the rehearsal room. A mirror, underclothes, and assortments of well-researched props, gloves, shoes, hats, can be left around, ready to be picked up and used in rehearsal, so that a costume becomes the actor's second skin. When the actors are not being used in a scene, I work with them in this room, learning from them the development of the character, rather than imposing on them a preconceived concept. Scenographic research exists in the past, present and future, and is an integral part of a good production.

I am a compulsive observer of human life and wherever I go I am watching and ferreting out tiny details that I can record and might be of use to me later. I never travel without a small sketchbook in my pocket that can be unobtrusively used to record the little details and idiosyncrasies that interest me. In Tbilisi, in Georgia, the old and the new rub shoulders in the streets. Fashionable women pass by old craftsmen working as they have done for hundred of years in the open air. While I was there I had the opportunity to travel into the mountain regions, as always armed with pen and paper. This whole area is made up of small fiefdoms with their own habits, customs and social structure. Georgian hospitality is legendary, and doors are always opened to visitors to come and share a four-hour lunch. This seemed such a rare opportunity to create a good aide-mémoire that I was anxious to record as much as possible, and in particular the striking looks and faces that spoke so eloquently of their turbulent history, knowing somewhere it would come to good use.

As I was working on a new production of Shakespeare's *Macbeth* I was watching the news on television. It was focused on the tiny Scottish island of Iona where the leader of the

Figure 3.1   Costume drawing for *Macbeth*, Theatr Clwyd

Labour Party in Great Britain, John Smith, was to be buried. This was the legendary burial place of King Duncan of Forres, whose murder at the hands of Macbeth starts the disastrous chain of events leading to death after death in the play. On television we saw the elliptical outline of Iona silhouetted against a luminous sky. As the funeral procession went to the grave the officiating priest from the Church of Scotland described the island as "a very thin place where only a tissue paper separates the material from the spiritual world". In *Macbeth* Shakespeare creates a world where the supernatural lives next to the natural, the two worlds inextricably linked. I immediately imagined a fragile thin curved shell-shaped stage that

could be lit from underneath, where the three weird sisters would live, and the mortal world would live above them. Remembering my Georgian drawings, that depicted similarly isolated clans in the Caucasus mountains, I saw how these two images could be used together to create the landscape for the play. No experience is ever wasted (Figure 3.1).

Occasionally life and art collide, giving the opportunity for research to take a personal focus that can inform a whole production. The play I least wanted to do, Shakespeare's *Merchant of Venice*, was offered to me, with the great actor Sir Alec Guinness playing Shylock. I have always felt this was an unnecessarily contentious play, no matter how good the production. 41

Even the eighteenth-century versions that tried to present it as a comedy failed to mask its deficiencies and difficulties. We met in his contemplative garden at his home in the Sussex countryside to talk about the issues of this play. In his house was a collection of reproduction Morandi paintings. One was a still life of bottles on a flat table against a blank wall. Each bottle was isolated and lonely, its shape and form pitilessly depicted with all its flaws, and thrown into prominence by the plain flat background wall. Morandi is a twentieth-century painter who seems timeless. His compositions, like those of Chardin, place objects in space with the precision and accuracy of a stage director, and they tell an unspoken story of fear and isolation. Alec Guinness said this picture was a key for him into the play. Walls keep people in and out, and define people as insiders or outsiders, which he saw as Shylock's very human predicament. He is needed to help the society he lives in to function, but is always excluded. We talked about the dilemma of minorities, and the modern parallels of ethnic divisions and imposed pass laws that consign selected people behind walls so that they may not contaminate or intermarry and pollute the rest of the population. The dangers of this are tragically depicted in Shakespeare's play. Alec Guinness's gentle, quietly spoken and reasoned observations greatly impressed me, and I decided to go to Venice to see exactly the world of the play, and the ghetto that Shakespeare had heard about but never seen. Of course *The Merchant of Venice* is not literally about Venice, and it is not necessary to reproduce Renaissance buildings on the stage. However, I was searching for an eloquent and appropriate metaphor, and this journey was no more than a starting point. It was freezing cold and wet when I arrived in Venice in the early spring and everything I saw there was no doubt coloured by the high fever I immediately contracted. Through a haze, I stumbled around with a small box of watercolours, a camera and one piece of information from a nineteeth-century guidebook. It said: "After April 1516 Venetian Jews were forced to settle in a separate district, in a former gietto [ghetto] or artillery foundry." The ghetto is in Sestriere on the Canale Canareggio and entered through a portico flanked by two ancient wooden watchtowers or customs houses opening onto a squalid and cramped square. The first astonishing surprise was how small the ground area was and how extraordinarily high and precarious the buildings are. Like so many shanty towns, where people can't build out they build up. This immediately pointed to a possible staging solution for the play: to contrast Venice (vertical and closed in) with Belmont (horizontal and open). Embedded into an old wall on the right of the entrance to the ghetto was a small ancient plaque written in Latin, listing the rules of the ghetto imposed by the Venetian court: when the gates would be opened and closed, the hours of the curfew, the requirement to carry identity at all times, prohibition on public gatherings and religious observances, and strict forbidding of association with Jews who had converted to Christianity and were therefore allowed to live outside the ghetto. This was Shylock's world. It was striking how many walls carried other edicts in deeply incised Roman lettering, and as the changing light caught the facets of the incisions, the letters became darker and darker. In an instant I had the whole image of the play before my eyes. I could make a wall of incised Roman lettering which would be the text in English of the Latin plaque at the ghetto entrance. The ghetto regulations would be ever-present, a constant reminder to Shylock of the restrictions of everyday life. To create the different Venice locations the wall could open, and each half could swing upstage creating different spaces of narrow streets, and small squares. For the contrasting Belmont scenes the wall could swing upstage and not be seen at all. I feverishly made small on-site sketches, and could not wait to get back to England to share these discoveries. At the first opportunity I went to meet the director, Patrick Garland, and Alec Guinness, and they immediately began to have ideas as to how they could use the wall. We looked for a long time at the work of the Romanian photographer Roman Vishniac. In these photographs of isolated figures cowering against old walls we found a parallel with the poignant isolation of Shylock in Venice (Figure 3.2). The atmosphere would be further intensified by using the plangent string music of the Shostakovich trios, played over the calm and religious Monteverdi Vespers. We all felt that this was a way through this difficult subject, where the subtext could be visually expressed without dominating the scene and drowning the actors. I was thankful I had not simply relied on second-hand information found in a book, but had really experienced and recorded at first hand the sinister atmosphere of the Venice ghetto.

Actual field research can yield very unexpected results, and wherever possible I have travelled to sites where plays are set, and have created a personal filing system where I can cross reference my visual information. This filing system is housed in a collection of shoeboxes which are the perfect size and shape for postcards and photographs, and are easily stacked on top of each other. Information is useless unless it can be easily retrieved. When preparing Federico García Lorca's *Yerma* I went to Andalucía to see if I could observe or sense some simple element that would sum up this strange enclosed world. I was staying in Granada, and planned to go to

SHYLOCK 1. ALEC GUINNESS MEF   OF VENICE CHICHESTER F. T
ANTIQUE BLACK AND GOLD TWISTED   SASH: 1984. A
BLACK TEXTURED UNDEROBE. DAMASK   RIBBED SILK WITH C.FASTENING :
RED FOX FUR HAT : BLUE/GREEN OVER —   COAT CUT ON CAFTAN SHAPE/SHOT FABRIC?

Figure 3.2   Costume drawing of Alec Guinness as Shylock, Chichester Festival Theatre

Viznar, the execution ground where Lorca died in 1936 and where, I had heard, a memorial park had been recently built in his memory. I had a map, but it was very unclear. I was with a Spanish speaker, and we quickly discovered that no-one wanted to tell us. There was a heavy and uneasy atmosphere in this small village. Eventually we found the deserted memorial garden, behind ornate black iron gates left half open. The garden was constructed as a layered courtyard with Lorca's poems hand painted onto tiles. Running water and fountains sprang from unseen sources in the secret hills above the tracks where lorries had rumbled at night, and the executions had taken place early in the morning overheard by the inhabitants of Viznar, so graphically described in the witnessed accounts contained in Ian Gibson's book *The Assassination of Federico García Lorca*. But in the memorial garden, the tiles were smashed, tins of paint and stones had been thrown against them, the silent walls of poems defiled. That night in Granada in a hot hotel room, I heard the dogs howling. The tension was unforgettable.

On my return, I remembered a similar journey I had made some years earlier to Sfad in Israel above Lake Tiberias, another enclosed community. I found my drawings and photographs in the appropriate shoe-box and saw that the walls were painted in the traditional cool green and blue, incised with designs of jasmine flowers as I had seen in Andalucía. The very small front doors were below street level, and above the blue painted arched doorways there were pieces of coloured glass embedded into the plaster catching the sunlight. The dark interiors were sparsely furnished, and venturing behind the façades of these secret houses I saw enormous quantities of white female underwear criss-crossing the small yards on old knotted ropes. The juxtaposition of these two experiences, Viznar and Sfad, became the environment for the production of *Yerma*, seen through the eyes of two women, the director Di Trevis and myself who could both understand Yerma's passionate desire for a child. In order to give total prominence to the performers, and to keep the production as simple as possible, we decided to make a theatre in the round. The two balconies of the Cottesloe Theatre, surrounding the space on four sides, were hung with women's white underwear, like the washing on the lines that I had seen. We made a cool green plaster floor, and when it was still wet in the paintshop drew into it an incised pattern of jasmine flowers. On this floor, supplemented only by minimal wooden furniture, terracotta ceramics and low-level lighting, the director created endless emotive pictures with the actors, who glided seamlessly from interior to exterior, capturing the many changing moods of the play and giving the audience an insight into what lay at the heart of the oppressive atmosphere of an enclosed female community.

Researching the medieval world of the play by Fernando de Rojas, *La Celestina*, and the cities where he is known to have lived, I went to Salamanca in Spain. *La Celestina* takes place in a small fictitious town, supposedly by the sea since the young heroine watches ships go by from her tower where she is enclosed. Salamanca is not by the sea, but is where the original manuscript is kept, and is where the autos-da-fé during the Spanish Inquisition were held. It is not difficult to see the medieval world of *La Celestina* in today's Salamanca, where, for their own safety, people were constantly on the move, running close to the walls and being careful not to be heard in public for "walls have ears". The play is written in constant movement, with no-one staying in one place for any length of time. Everyone is suspicious, wary and nervous. My days in Salamanca were dark, heavy and thunderous, punctuated by sonorous church bells tolling continuously, adding to the oppressive atmosphere. It seemed airless, as if the sun could not rise high enough over the towers of the buildings. Then I saw the walls of the university, covered with graffiti dating from the fifteenth century to the present day. In extraordinary graphic writing decorated with little moons and stars, students names, slogans, and statements were painted on the exterior of the university, as if the very spirit of the people was rising up against the walls (Figure 3.3). I stood in the street and drew this for future use. Nothing is ever wasted.

Our intimate lives and secrets are revealed in what we discard. Rubbish skips are a never-ending source of inspiration for the magpie scenographer. We pick over other people's trash for things that we may be able to use, and this too is research. Thrift shops all over the world are magnets for researchers who want to see and feel how clothes were made, and study the way that decorations changed from the days of hand crafting to the wartime utility clothes. These details can still be found in markets and small towns, although many antique clothes have become collectables, and are rapidly rising in value. Costumes and clothes throughout the ages reflect the moral and cultural climate of the time. The visual style of a period invades everything from personal dress to public buildings. What we wear is rarely neutral. Most articles of clothing proclaim their period and reflect the current architecture, style, and taste. The perpendicular construction of early churches, with soaring stone arches and pillars, is echoed in the flowing perpendicular folds of the medieval portraits of elongated knights and their ladies. The English Tudor low arches seen in the

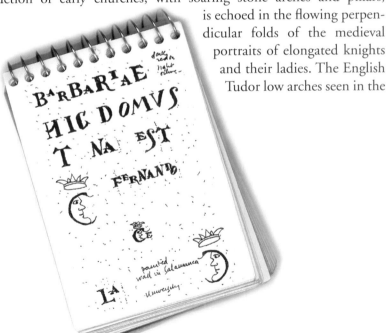

46   Figure 3.3   On-site sketches of the writing on the university walls, Salamanca

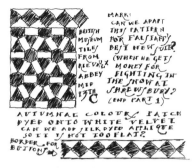

Figure 3.4   Medieval tile pattern research drawing

great Elizabethan palaces are carried on the portraits of the coiffured ladies, their hooped and draped robes filling the architectural spaces in perfect harmony. Rounded arches are echoed in the rounded skirts of the eighteenth-century, wooden and stone floral and decorative carvings being interpreted exactly in ribbons and silks. These examples are repeated in every period, and the current movement of eclectic forms and deconstructed temporary architecture is mirrored in the everyday dress in high streets all over the world. Period clothes can be customised to reflect the idiosyncrasies of the wearer, through the choice of pattern, decoration ornaments, and material and the way the garment is worn. We can take and mix periods and styles if it feels right for the play

Figure 3.5   Costume drawing of Timothy West as Falstaff, using the tile pattern

or the character. Cross-referencing and transferring research is creative as long as it adds to the clarity of the character. I have used a tile pattern from a medieval pavement seen in the British Museum (Figure 3.4) and turned it into a printed textile for one of Falstaff's costumes (Figure 3.5), and by contrast used a modern biker's leather jacket for an Elizabethan doublet in *The Revenger's Tragedy*.

Fascinating as it is, researching a piece of work can also be a trap, where the research becomes more interesting than the play itself. Programmes become small books, lavishly illustrated with the fruits of the research, archive photographs of previous productions and erudite semi-academic articles. It is a grim warning to sit in the audience and become aware that more people are reading the programme than watching the performance in front of them. Research is only the medium through which the play can take its shape, colour and form, and should be able to be absorbed into the work so that it becomes quite natural for everyone to feel themselves in the world of the play. Bringing the research into the rehearsal room as an active ingredient of the group work, and not just making it a private activity, helps everyone to live the parts of the play, and for the short period of that particular work become an "expert" on the subject. Surprising memories come forward, that probably have lain dormant for years just waiting for an opportunity to be used.

Working on a new production of Anton Chekhov's 1904 masterpiece *The Cherry Orchard* with the director Stephen Unwin, I remembered nearly thirty years previously, on my first visit to Poland, being taken into the Mazovian countryside to visit a small manor house, very dilapidated, called Żelazowa Wola. This house, built in 1820, was the birth-place of the composer and pianist Frédéric Chopin, who spent much of his life travelling between Poland and Paris. The white cherry blossoms that surrounded the house were in full bloom, and cast shadows over the old white plaster walls. All the interlocking rooms were identically decorated, with windows looking out onto the cherry orchard. The severity was only relieved by a continuous series of dark-brown wooden curved lintels over the windows, from which hung tattered remnants of curtains. The wooden floor had faded to near white, and white double doors spoke of a grander time in the past. It conveyed an unforgettable enchanting simplicity, an image that had already imprinted itself onto my memory for future use, for a scenographer collects images as a writer collects dialogue (Figures 3.6, 3.7).

I wrote down the following poem from the back of the guide book:

leaves with their dry whisperings
bring so many thoughts,
and so many memories,
and so much music

That's research – a voyage of discovery.

Figure 3.6   Sketch for *The Cherry Orchard*

Figure 3.7   Sketch for *The Cherry Orchard*

CHAPTER 4

COLOUR AND COMPOSITION
The Balancing Act

Colour and composition are the crux of the scenographer's art. When the text has been researched and the playing space is known, the next challenge for the scenographer is to compose and colour the playing space, with figures and forms creating a visual envelope for the performance. Everything on the stage, fixed or moving, is part of this kinetic composition. The integration of composition with colour enables the artist to draw the spectator's eye to the focal points of each scene as the performance progresses. In creating a satisfying composition the scenographer has to both see and feel the space. Becoming the master of the space gives freedom to play with size and colour, so that, as in a still life painting, the selected objects are transformed. The spectator sees through the artist's eye what has been included in order to tell the story, and can imagine what is implied.

Objects and elements do not speak by themselves. They must be placed in a relationship to the space, and to each other, in order to have an eloquence and meaning. Then they talk to each other across the empty space. The way the image is placed transforms actuality into art. In a stage composition, the object is much more than its literal self. It becomes an emblem for the hidden world of the play, something that lies behind but supports the player's words. Its power and appropriateness will carry a significance beyond what it appears to be, as well as a satisfying sense of beauty and authority. The objective is to create visual images that captivate the theatre spectator. A visitor to an art gallery has the freedom to move slowly or pass swiftly from painting to painting, depending on their personal interest. The exhibits are static and do not change. In the theatre, the spectator is static, and the stage is constantly changing its visual images through a combination of colour and composition.

The scenographic composition that unfolds to the spectator should unify performers and objects in a series of poetic statements that capture the essence of truth and reality and offer both recognition and surprise. This does not depend only on the subject, either factual or abstract, but is related to the placing of the image on the paper, or within the volume of the stage space. The scenic composition may start on paper as an idea in two dimensions, but then has to prove itself when translated into three dimensions. Testing ideas in a maquette helps this transference and makes clear where to place the elements that construct the image of the play and how to use colour imaginatively and evocatively. The empty space is simultaneously a two- and three-dimensional experience.

The use of colour within a pictorial composition is like a composer's choice of musical scale. Once the key is set, and the extremes at either end of the scale are fixed, all the choices fit at intervals in between. In the same way that shapes and forms balance within a space, so do colours. Colour guides the viewer's eye to the focal point and meaning of a composition through careful placing within a space, or frame. Understanding colour is often a trick of the eye. What may be perceived by the viewer from a distance as a single colour may well be made up of many colours only visible close up. Studying the way the viewer reads 'green', an overexposed everyday colour, by looking at landscapes reveals a huge variety of methods of depicting fields and trees, and how many colours can appear to be green just by their juxtaposition to each other.

Edvard Munch, in his painting *The Dance of Life*, employed a highly charged and emotive use of colour to depict the drama of the subject. The colour range is very limited, giving a sombre and uniquely Nordic atmosphere. The picture shows a group of people together yet isolated, the spaces between them being painted in a strong vibrant green more intense than the centrally placed red-dressed woman. Framing the picture are two female figures without dancing partners, one dressed in white, the other in a very dark green, almost black. The figure in white holds her arms open as if waiting for an absent partner. Opposite her, the dark woman's head is bowed, her hands firmly clasped together. The shapes of the four other dancers dressed in white seem like pieces of paper fluttering to the ground. The white moon throws a vertical beam reflected in a horizontal lake placed off centre, and suggests an altar on which a sacrifice may be made.

Use of colour to summarise and evoke the emotional life of a play is often my first and most truthful reaction to a text. It can be used to release the emotional resonance of the play. At the beginning of my work on Ibsen's *Hedda Gabler*, for a new production directed by Stephen Unwin, with a specially commissioned translation by Kenneth McLeish, I dreamt of a dark green empty room in which stark isolated figures were thrown into sharp relief by a strong light from a distant outside world. I realised how like Munch's *The Dance of Life* this was. This painting echoes the sombre mood of *Hedda Gabler* in which the stage directions describe a room decorated in dark colours with an inner room concealed behind curtains. Working on the first draft of the maquette with the director, I decided to try using the most restricted palette possible, and to see how many variations I could make on four or five colours. I used a flat dark-green for all the walls, and tried emphasising the colour by framing the base of the walls with a natural polished parquet floor and the top with a similarly coloured decorative wooden beam. The only other colours were dark-red, dark-blue, black and a light parchment colour, which were used on all the furniture and costumes. The composition began to take on a landscape proportion which at first seemed to work against the portrait shape of most theatres. Later, as we experimented with setting the walls at an angle to the front of the stage, we saw how combining two opposite forms can produce a visual and dramatic tension that intrigues and engages the spectator. Although it is not my favourite occupation, I find it absolutely necessary, when working in the maquette, to make carefully and beautifully to scale all the furniture the play requires. Only like this can the director and I move the pieces around and create really telling colour compositions that mirror the tone of the words. I consider the shape, size and quality of each item of furniture as a sculptural object to be carefully chosen and correctly placed.

Using colour, experimenting with different types and combinations of media to achieve just the right feel, is utterly pleasurable. The choice of media can capture the feeling of the words or music. I use inks and acrylics, watercolour and crayons, and often search out heavy duty paints made for industrial use. For all the walls and floor of Ibsen's *The Masterbuilder* I used a high gloss grey-blue paint developed for boats, with small accents of a flat terracotta paint used to rust-proof iron girders, both on the maquette and in the final stage version. The grey-blue colour was thickly painted over wooden planked walls and wide wooden floorboards, researched from period architectural books of speculative builders' patterns for turn-of-the-century Norwegian "homes for ordinary people". The potential heaviness of the grey-blue was offset by two framed doorways on either side of the stage painted in a thin, off-white, water-based paint. The wall surfaces were highly reflective and bounced the light back onto the actors, causing them to stand out in sharp relief and be seen with a crystal-like clarity that was the hallmark of the translation.

Colour speaks. Not only can it be used to accent objects within a composition, it can also unify a free or non-traditional theatre space. The bold use of one colour is very evocative, and powerful, and a simple way of creating a strong statement. Sometimes the characteristics of a space, its walls and floor, and the atmosphere it generates, can simply suggest a dominant colour by imagining what could look good and effective, and then seeing if that instinct has any validity against the needs of the production. I have imagined a huge, yellow, curved wall for a big open stage, a brilliant ultramarine blue in a proscenium stage, and in the redbrick Tramway theatre a sharp green colour danced before my eyes. This huge rectangular shell of a performance space forty-two metres long by twenty-six metres wide has four terracotta brick walls rising seven and a half metres to a wooden pitched roof. Two walls at right angles to the side walls at one end form a natural brick proscenium opening, backed with a matching terracotta plaster wall serving as a flat cyclorama. The four side walls have many recessed arches that break up the surface area and create dramatic shadows, and the brown wooden roof is supported by two rows of black iron pillars running through the centre of the space. Unifying this space was one of the visual challenges when we began work on the sequel to John McGrath's *Border Warfare* – an original "work play" entitled *John Brown's Body* in which the scenes were visualised as they were written. The production of *John Brown's Body*, an epic story of Scotland's fortunes and misfortunes from the eighteenth century to the present day, had to incorporate a folk music band, and was also to be made into a three-part television film. All the visual ideas, costumes and props had to be both stage-worthy and camera-ready. Having done one promenade production in this venue we wanted to profit from that experience, not repeat a formula but to develop more techniques of highly visual and presentational "event telling". We looked at the walls of the building, with their bricked-up recessed arches, and wondered if we could build stages round the walls, using the red bricks as the principal background colour, and incorporate several acting areas at eye level, at least one metre off the ground, so that a standing audience of 600 could see. I was very doubtful as to how this could be achieved. From the structure of the narrative came certain imperatives. The suggestion of a rural world had to stay throughout as a poignant reminder of what was lost when a pastoral and agricultural society became industrialised and fields turned into factories. The story started in the mid eighteenth-century and finished in the consumer multi-national society of the present post-industrial age. John McGrath said one day, casually, "Life is like a roller coaster" and that phrase must have stayed somewhere in my mind as the project began to take shape. In order to start, and make some reasonably practical drawings, I photographed the Tram-way walls and then enlarged them to 1:50 scale. I then put the photographs together edge to edge, flattening out the rectangle of the building so that it resembled a medieval cartoon like the passion plays performed in the streets. In this way I could see the dimensions of the problem, with the four segments of vast empty wall laid end to end. I then overpainted the pho-tographs and textured them to give as much of the colour and atmosphere of the building as possible. Not quite knowing what to do, I idly took a length of thin string that just happened to be near at hand, painted it bright green, and laid it across the long, narrow, painted photograph of the Tramway walls. As it fell naturally in curves and rises, it seemed to bind together the walls and disparate spaces with a single strong band of colour. Suddenly the green line spoke to me of the remembered Elysian fields of pastoral Scotland that were in the text, and it also had the up-and-down movement of a roller coaster, the subtext of the fortunes and misfortunes of the country. As I moved the string higher up the painting I saw how it could be constructed as the green runway all round the walls that I had been so doubtful about initially. The script had suggested a two-level stage, with the "aristocratic" and "power" scenes played on the upper level and small stages below for the band and the industrial scenes. The visual com-position would reproduce the structure of the text. I had recently been on a visit to Russia, and had been looking at the constructivist paintings in the Russian Museum. I suddenly saw how the dynamism and the sharp angular forms of these early paintings could be reinterpreted as the struc-ture for our stages. But most importantly I fell in love with the colour of the piece of green string against the terracotta of the walls, and began to imagine other secondary colours that would also look powerful – shining-black, brilliant blue, and an industrial gloss red. In a fever of excitement we began talking and designing, writer/director and scenographer, creating instant images of industrial machinery, a fairground with a giant ferris wheel, a prison, a factory, a farm, a train – in fact we found we could create anything we wanted in this space. Although it was on a large scale, 55

the vision for *John Brown's Body* was strong and simple, able to withstand the many compromises that present themselves as time and money come into the equation. But the piece of green string remained the most important unifying visual element, and was a clear symbol for the heart of the production, providing the three-dimensional frame for the composition of all the scenic elements required by the piece. Creating the photographic collage of the Tramway like a medieval tableau enabled everyone to imagine the progression of the production as it moved around the walls of the building. It also enabled the linear composition of each wall to be balanced against its opposite wall so that there was a variety within a whole concept.

This balance and harmony of composition is well illustrated in the study of medieval illuminated manuscripts. On one plain rectangular page, image and text are completely interwoven with breathtaking leaps of the imagination.

The images are carefully placed on the vellum to catch the light and to illuminate the story, creating a desire for the reader to turn to the next page. More glorious colour combinations than could be dreamt of bring fantastic animals and birds to life on the page, each one more surprising than the last. Every possibility within the page is used to the maximum to create the most compelling iconography, that is at once decorative and beautiful, powered by the belief in the importance of celebrating and retelling a well-known story.

This motivation can also be seen in the work of original folk artists all over the world, who inherit a tradition of colour, shape and form, and

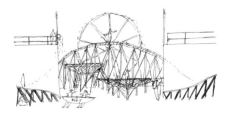

are able to retain a decorative simplicity even when adapting their skills for sophisticated uses. The great Polish artist, puppeteer, and scenographer Adam Kilian is a vivid example of how to use simple and elemental design in a powerful contemporary manner. On a visit to Kilian's studio, the door opened on a riot of drawings, paintings and theatre posters he had designed pinned to every conceivable surface. He was surrounded by a magical world of masks, painted wooden birds, wooden puppets, and brilliantly traditional Polish coloured paper cut-outs, which served as research for his work. There were numerous models of settings for national theatres and opera houses, as well as the small puppet theatres he adored. I asked him to explain to me, in the midst of this jumble, what he was doing. He replied, "Composing! That's what a scenographer does. Compose with colour and form! It's the most beautiful and exciting thing to do, because so many people enjoy it." He took out a huge pair of scissors and proceeded to demonstrate with a large piece of thin red paper, which he folded many times. He made quick, tiny triangular, circular, rectangular cuts, working with amazing speed, literally drawing into the paper with scissors. He took another smaller sheet of yellow and did the same, and yet another smaller sheet of green paper and cut in the same way. He opened them out flat on his work table, sweeping books, pencils, drawings to the already littered floor, and laying green over yellow over red, showed me a fantastic picture of flowers, patterns, hens, and hearts, balanced in perfect harmony. He said that ordinary people from centuries past had taken inspiration and reference from nature – the everyday patterns of folk art that served both a functional and decorative purpose. I noticed that in these examples of Polish folk art, like the Japanese Kabuki Theatre, glaring primary colours were used in juxtaposition to each other, creating a disharmony, then counterbalanced by small blocks of subtle secondary colours, the whole contained within the precise form of the composition.

Some years after this memorable visit to Poland I used this experience for a production of Shakespeare's *As You Like It*. Remembering Kilian's genius with large scissors and coloured paper, I began to experiment with folding and cutting paper to make tree shapes, adding removable highly coloured birds and flowers, thinking the Forest of Arden could depict the changing seasons by first showing the unadorned tree shapes harshly backlit for the winter scenes, and then adding the birds and flowers for a colourful summer finale (Figure 4.1). The trees could be on hidden wheels, so that they could be regrouped to indicate different parts of the forest, and the paper cut-outs of the maquette interpreted in full size would be constructed from sheets of cut out plywood. On the stage, the white paper of the original designs became a white perspex box and floor, with actors' entrances concealed within it. It could be lit with different colours from

Figure 4.1   Drawing for *As You Like It*

behind and in front, and made to look like cold winter or warmer summer
at the end. The forest could disappear behind the perspex box, as a distant
backlit shadow, or come forward into the box for the forest scenes. This
was the beginning of a long pursuit of creating "plasticity" – movable
elements – in the composition of the stage space.

On that visit to Poland, Adam Kilian had shown me a familiar small
paint-stained postcard of Jean-Siméon Chardin's *A Jar of Apricots* (1758)
and said the remarkable thing about that painting was Chardin's understanding of French ceramic art shown on the two teacups in the foreground
of the painting. There is no background to this series of still-life paintings,
and the shapes of the objects, and their relationship to each other are the
composition. The painting celebrates the beauty of the ordinary domestic
object and by painting a second teacup in dark shadow in the background
the front cup is thrown into sharp relief. Their white-and-red flowered
pattern catches the viewer's attention, and leads the eye through the
painting to the focus: the deep, deep orange of the apricots in the jar, and
the space above, behind and around them. I knew this postcard very well.
I first met it as an art student when I was struggling to understand what
pictorial composition was and how it could be applied to theatre design. I
was fortunate at the age of sixteen to be a lowly assistant in a theatre paint

shop, mostly cleaning paint buckets but also the pupil of a dedicated teacher, artist and theatre designer who taught by practical example rather than theory. He loved still-life paintings, and through his enthusiasm I love them too. He gave me the Chardin postcard, introducing me to the miracle of paint and astonishing colour and composition. This small oval painting embodies beauty in everyday practical objects, which, when reassembled through the artist's eye, gives the spectator an entirely fresh viewpoint. These still-life paintings, like a stage composition, have an in-built geometry of interlocking planes linked only by the mysterious background colour. The shapes and forms flow into each other, leaving enigmatic spaces for the viewer's imagination to complete. Possessing this postcard then led me to look at other examples and I began a lifelong admiration for those artists who so naturally could create a sense of untold drama – telling a story through colour and composition. Dutch still-life paintings showed how everyday objects and people could hold a dramatic space with tension and expectation. The arrangement of planes, forms, and rectangles holds a metaphysical quality of stillness. Spanish still-life paintings concentrate even more on the assemblage of objects, fruit, fish and vegetables, enhancing them with light from an unseen source that endows them with a life of their own. I learned by doing. I would come into the theatre workshops, where I was both studying art and learning the practicalities of theatre, and discover a note left for me by my teacher. This would direct me to a corner of the workshop where a "still-life arrangement" would have been constructed for me to draw. This normally consisted of old telephone directories, some discarded theatre props, some half-eaten sandwiches, and perhaps a fake antique or two. The note would suggest I should draw the still life in a spare moment, and then look in the book of Dutch and Spanish still-life paintings and find which painting it represented by observing its composition rather than its content. This simple exercise of self-discovery opened my mind to looking at paintings and was the best art education I ever had, and has become part of my visual and scenographic vocabulary.

Being aware of the importance of both colour and composition when creating a stage picture depends on possessing and developing a critical ability – the really essential talent. Anyone can learn to draw, or paint, but it is much more difficult to acquire the skill to look at the result, question it and know how to alter it. Developing this critical awareness enables an artist to make decisions during the creative process. When the finished work finally reaches the public domain it is an accumulation of many small decisions, some instinctive but all continuously evaluated, until, to the best of the artist's ability, it seems to be "just right". The uniqueness of art education is based on acquiring a practised critical eye in the give and take of open group criticisms with fellow students. Having to look at one's work objectively through other people's eyes, is exactly what happens in the theatre, where often hundreds of pairs of eyes look at months of hard work for no more than three hours and think they could do it better. The art training that is essential for scenographers provides the common vocabulary for discussions about the balance of light against dark, the contrast of verticals, horizontals, and diagonals, the placing and interlocking of forms, and the judicious use of colour, all of which are the equivalent in composition to the plot line of the text.

The ability to understand the structure of pictorial and object composition, and how colour is linked, is the special contribution that a scenographer can bring to the theatre production and demonstrates clearly the interrelation between theatre and fine art. There are many examples, particularly in theatre history, in the twentieth-century. Russian pioneers such as Meyerhold, Vhaktangov, Tairov, and particularly Diaghilev, commissioned Picasso, Chagall, Gontachorova and so many others to create colourful compositions for the Ballets Russes that could exist as art works in their own right. The set and costume designs of the Russian painter and stage designer Léon Bakst, working with Diaghilev and the Ballets Russes from 1911, rework elements of folk, oriental and western art, and like the medieval manuscript illuminators create fantastical and swirling patterns and compositions. Bakst manipulates the human body across the diagonal of the paper, and counterbalances it with lengths of materials and extraordinary colours often overlaid and seen through each other. The negative spaces of the white ground paper left around the dancer's body are as strong and pulsating as the figure itself. Outstretched arms balance the width of a skirt, and the composition is often completed by a strong vertical staff or serpent boldly running up the side of the paper and turning back on itself into the body of the composition. Ignoring the content of the picture, Bakst is revealed as an artist who loved to play with paint and colour, counterbalancing interlocking curved and straight lines and contrasting geometric shapes. His works are as much about placing the design on the paper as describing the costume, and now have the value of truly collectable art.

In the Menil Foundation in Houston, USA, is a fine collection of paintings and theatre designs by the French theatre designer Christian

Bérard that are a complete contrast to the work of Bakst, though they contain many common points. Bérard created delicate, almost weightless, stage pictures that suggested, but never reproduced, the subject. He avoided strong colours, believing that they "worked to the detriment of the ear", and thought "the most important thing for the designer is to get the armature of the stage picture just right and to leave out as much as possible".[1] Despite his facility as a fine artist, his theatre work was three-dimensional, and he was famous for looking at the stage constantly from all the extreme seats in the house. His fine-art sensibilities enabled him to judge the weight, tone and impact of every costume on its own, and in relationship to each other, and to know when to enhance a colour with extra light or when to leave well alone.

The structures of fine art compositions are a helpful reference point for translating into contemporary plays. Tennessee Williams' play *The Rose Tattoo* is set in a small house in a Sicilian community near a highway in America. His evocative stage description asks "to show these gaudy child-like mysteries with sentiment and humour in equal measure, without ridicule and with respect for the religious yearnings they symbolise". I remembered Giovanni Battista Tiepolo's altarpiece of The Immaculate Conception, painted in 1769. It has a triangular structure, and at its apex the central figure of the Madonna is standing within a rectangular frame. The eye is taken to the very top of the painting by a small hovering white dove, the holy spirit, placed above the Madonna's head and linked by a barely perceptible shaft of light. This central image is surrounded by balanced and counterbalanced angels forming the two sides of the unseen triangle. They are not symmetrical and show how many different ways there are of repeating the same motif. This was exactly the inspiration I needed to show the world of the widow Serafina and her beloved daughter Rosa. Although it is set in modern-day America, it is a transposed Sicilian society, surrounded by neighbours, superstition and religious faith, much as it would have been back home. Planning the production, with the Polish/British director Helena Kaut Howson and some actors from the Theatre de Complicité, I chanced upon some large sheets of pink Indian handmade paper that suggested to me the colour of roses. I started to build a picture, drawing with a thin red pen. I imagined that seeing into this house would be like seeing into a woman's soul, and the house would be

---

1   Boris Kochno, *Christian Bérard* (ed. John Russell), London: Thames and Hudson, 1988.

Figure 4.2   Structural sketch based on
Tiepolo composition

an altar to her past life that is only alluded to in the play. Within a small and shabby exterior this would be a palace of colour, and a wall of memories of her marriage and Rosa's childhood, all imbued by pink, as if seen through rose-tinted glasses. The plot of the play moves very quickly from interior to exterior, so the director's idea to put the whole house on a revolving stage seemed to answer the author's suggestion of a house like a fairground carousel. It also gave the actors, well trained in physical theatre skill, opportunities to combine movement with music and become part of the scene-changing device. I began to build a picture based on the Tiepolo composition (Figure 4.2) by drawing Serafina sitting on a pink sofa like the centre of a rose, placed on a circular green carpet like its calyx (Figure 4.3). Above her head is a small Madonna lit by a decorative light, suspended from an ethereal semi-transparent rose. She is surrounded by the objects of her life – on one side, headless mannequins with half-made dresses, and on the other side heavy Sicilian-type furniture from her former life. Within the triangular shape of the small weatherboard house, all the forms of the furniture and objects are curved and circular. Her own world is shown to be in direct contrast to her external environment. This highly coloured "memory-altar" was always surrounded by black-clad neighbours who were watching as another on-stage audience from outside, emphasising the circular composition and providing the base of the unseen triangle. Tennessee Williams describes his play as an ascension play, and at the last moment the truck driver Mangiacavallo, now Serafina's saviour and lover, climbs up onto the rooftop and throws his red silk shirt up to heaven. Transferring the composition of the Tiepolo to Tennessee Williams made a structural cross-connection that gave a strength and weight to the *mise en scène* of *The Rose Tattoo*. The exterior of the house was on the reverse side of the interior and revolved into view. The wooden weatherboard

Figure 4.3   Sketch for *The Rose Tattoo*

walls, overhanging porch, deck and fencing were undercoated with a strong, red gloss paint then overbrushed with a flat, thin white paint, resulting in a faint rosy glow capturing the quality of the original design. The colour, movement of the revolve and composition brought forward clearly the original idea of showing the heart of this woman as if it were a bright and colourful carousel of memories set in the alien hard concrete world of urban America. Tennessee Williams wrote *The Rose Tattoo* in 1950, and described it as "poetic realism" – a genre of plays in which time is suspended and confined to the stage. He describes the theatre experience as thus: "For a couple of hours we surrender ourselves to a world of fiercely illuminated values in conflict", and suggests that because the audience only watches these conflicts on stage, without needing to be involved or participate in their resolution, we can indulge in "the almost liquid warmth of unchecked human sympathies".

In Great Britain at this time, new ideas and new writers were emerging, moving away from the illusionistic stage naturalism of the post-war years into a theatre of poetic contemporary images. To complement this new writing, ideas about design were also undergoing a major change,   63 spearheaded by the woman scenepainter-turned-designer Jocelyn Herbert, who became the most influential figure in the new theatre, and the first British scenographer. Jocelyn Herbert had seen Bertolt Brecht's productions of *The Caucasian Chalk Circle* and *Mother Courage*, and recreated in London *The Good Person of Setzuan* from the original designs that Teo Otto had made with Brecht in Zürich in 1942. She was impressed by the simplicity and quality of the Berliner Ensemble, attributable not only to Brecht himself but to the painter-designer who inspired him from the beginning, Caspar Neher; Brecht's later work was much influenced by that of Karl von Appen. Jocelyn Herbert began a lifetime of influential searching to create an equivalent form of poetic realism on the stage, and in so doing influenced a generation of scenographers, bringing new lifeblood to the British theatre. Her gifts of drawing, common sense and practicality enabled her to make stage compositions of chairs and tables, walls and washing lines of incomparable beauty. She used all the possibilities of the Royal Court Theatre stage, including incorporating the pipes and radiators on the back wall of the theatre into the composition for Arnold Wesker's *The Kitchen*. The lighting rig was always visible, and was included in the drawings as an integral part of the stage picture. Jocelyn Herbert paid great attention to art exhibitions and paintings, using them as reference sources, always finding modern equivalent interpretations. She used colour sparingly, often placing sharp accents within the overall composition if a particular object needed the audience's attention. She responded visually to George Devine's wish for the Royal Court Theatre to "clear the stage, and let in the light and air".

In 1965 the Berliner Ensemble came to London with *Coriolanus*, *The Threepenny Opera* and *Arturo Ui*. This was a memorable moment for everyone who saw these productions, not only also for the content of the plays, but for their astonishingly clear and beautiful *mise en scène*. For the first time we saw the power of the visual symbol on the stage, how it was presented and how colour could be used emotively. The plays were designed by Karl von Appen, and were dramatic in their observation and portrayal of truthful personal detail set against a larger epic background. In Brecht's version of Shakespeare's *Coriolanus*, the huge city walls were built on a revolve. Everything on the stage was painted in tones of grey, and the costumes echoed this theme. There was a wealth of personal detail within each uniform that let the audience believe that each soldier was also a mother's son, with a history of his own. Suddenly Coriolanus's mother Volumnia arrived through the central door. The tiny figure of Hélène

Weigel, Brecht's widow, was dressed in a simple but stunning scarlet robe. With one streak of colour, centrally placed, framed by the composition of the grey-clad soldiers on either side, it was immediately clear that it was she who held the power and not her son. The Berliner Ensemble demonstrated a new method of using colour and composition, working from the actor outwards by using indicative but imagined locales, encouraging the audience to believe what they could see and to imagine what they could not. This was the break from stage-painted naturalism, to using the stage as Brecht and Neher described – "to make a significant statement about reality" – by working on the essentials of the play, finding out what the players really needed, what was happening to and through them, and composing an eloquent response in colour and form.

Caspar Neher loved drawing, and was extremely quick and fluent. He had a retentive visual memory, and was able to transpose useful images from his own experience into stage images. His early unused watercolour sketches for Brecht's *Mother Courage* seem to echo his days in the Bavarian Field Artillery during the First World War, when despite being on active manouevres he was constantly painting from the small box of watercolours he carried everywhere with him. These two drawings, done after the war, take the form of a horizontal landscape with a high horizon line, a feature of many Neher compositions. In the first picture there is an empty waste-land, with a group of dark-clad soldiers, their armaments angled towards the centre forming a vertical line. The focus is Yvette the camp whore dressed in white, and she is framed at the other side by another vertical dark figure, small but placed at the very edge of the composition. This exquisite sketch of the empty battlefield, in which people form the elements of the landscape, seems to speak for all wars and all times. The second picture is a variation on this composition. Neher retains the horizontal format but adds a simple wooden fence placed on the diagonal across the stage, creating a split staging. The dynamic of the space is altered, and, by dividing it, allows the spectator to see two actions at the same time while becoming aware of the difference in status between people on either side of the fence. Caspar Neher incorporates into his composition the political and philosophical ethos that was the *raison d'être* for his commitment to collaborating with his "brother in arte" Bertolt Brecht.

Brecht greatly admired Neher's pragmatic and workmanlike approach to art, that demonstrated that art and aesthetics have an important role to play despite the discomfort and trials of war, and he records this admiration in his poem "About a Painter". Like many artists Caspar Neher simply painted or drew something everyday, no matter what the circumstances and with whatever materials came to hand. This ordinariness, this consistent practice, sharpens and develops the continuing search to understand the enigma of composition with colour that is the structure of art. Just as a musician practises scales and technical exercises daily before embarking on large-scale works, or a dancer works out daily at the barre, so the visual artist works to achieve fluency of line, colour, and the placing of a shape or object in a space. It sounds so simple, but there are infinite variations and possibilities, and often it is helped by a collaborator's eye seeing when a composition is "just right". That is the beauty of the shared experience of theatre work. Not only can the artist be inspired and motivated by the lines of a text, but so can a writer be inspired by the quality of a line or the intensity of a colour.

In Brecht's poem about Caspar Neher, "The Friends", he defines the importance of colour and composition, while walking through a destroyed city:

> *The cities where we worked are no longer there.*
> *When I walk through the cities that still are*
> *At times I say: that blue piece of washing*
> *My friend would have placed it better.*

CHAPTER 5

DIRECTION Finding the Way

The direction of a production makes a vision of the unknown become known through the collaboration of its creative artists: the director, writer, scenographer, choreographer, and lighting designer. From their different perspectives, they come together to plan the structure of a production that will be brought to life on the stage by the performers. Collaboration is more than an ideal – it is the most important creative force that enables ideas to be discussed and battled for and eventually to be coherently realised. Normally the final decisions rest with the director, whose overall vision leads the direction of the production. Sometimes the director is also the writer or the scenographer, but the important point is that each person in the creative team has an independent and interrelated part to play. The theatre director and director of the Old Vic Theatre School, Michel Saint-Denis, always stated that "People who work in theatre should know how to value the work of each person involved, and what it entails, whatever their department." There has to be a clear vision, and ideas for the production have to be tried and tested from all points of view, conceptual, aesthetic and practical. Nothing should be out of balance. Collaboration is the battle for harmony on the stage, in which all the players share and seek contributions from each other in order to gain strength through unity.

The first meeting between the director and the scenographer is often where all the foundations for the work to come are laid. The most important reaction at this delicate first moment is for the scenographer to be excited and intrigued by the project, to be a good listener, and to hear the reasons for choosing this particular play at this particular time, its context, who will be in it, and what direction the work might take. The director and scenographer have to decide at this early stage what they want the   67

Figure 5.1 Collage sheet recording discussions with the director for the staging of *The Masterbuilder*

spectator to understand and take away from the production. This is the measuring tool for all the subjective artistic decisions to be taken. Both the scenographer and the director have to try to view their proposals objectively, imagining that they are also the spectators, who have not read or studied the play, but are receiving the culmination of months of detailed work once only, in the space of two or three hours. It is a rigorous test, that has to be applied to every aspect of the production, where so much can be implied and suggested without being directly spoken. This is the launching pad of the production. Surprisingly, the best work does not always come from immediately falling in love with the play. Sometimes the richest experience comes after a real battle to understand the text, get to know it, and to discover how to unlock its closed and sometimes impenetrable doors. A judicious combination of people, perhaps not always in agreement, who can bring different and unexpected skills to the project is a good recipe for success.

At the all-important first meeting, I simply listen and make notes in a list on the first page of a new sketch book bought especially for the project. When discussing the future work on Ibsen's *Masterbuilder* I wrote the following while the director, Stephen Unwin, talked:

> freshness; like a new play; clear; a poet of the theatre; language of ordinary speech; real people; imagined stage image; recreate the stage directions; trust the writing; not Victorian England; Oslo far north; provincial; moral; social democrats; homes for ordinary people; visionary realist; fantasy; God; darkness; paradox; grey/blue; uncomfortable; Nietzsche; symbolic; precise; uncluttered; shapes in sharp relief; strong directional light; halo; aura; space; claustrophobia; Japanese screens [see Figure 5.1].

In subsequent weeks, as the direction of the production evolved through many discussions, versions of models and drawings, I hardly referred to this list or remembered it was there. Yet looking at the final production on stage I was aware that it clearly contained everything we had said in that first tentative meeting. Often the first ideas are the best ideas, but they have to be proved to be so by exploring all possible avenues, and, through a joint process of elimination between director and scenographer, earn their place on the stage.

To be successful the boundaries between director and scenographer have to be subtly interwoven, so that they are invisible to the spectator. These boundaries are greatly affected by the use of the dramatic space. In a truly fruitful and collaborative creation the scenographer works alongside the director to make the space speak through the performers. Good collaboration between the two is the heart of successful theatre-making. Both need to show respect for each other's artistic abilities in order to put their joint thoughts and ideas into practice. Scenography and direction should work together like two halves of a brain, the visual and spatial talents of the scenographer complementing and working with the literary and narrative talents of a director to form the course the production will take. Direction is the vision that everyone involved in creating the production has agreed to work towards.

How this can be achieved is easily demonstrated through drawings that pinpoint the important plot moments in which the disposition of the stage space is as eloquent as the speeches the characters make within it. The drawings laid out on the production desk and on the walls of the rehearsal studio in a Living Museum are a guide for everyone to explore and deviate from as the story of the play unfolds and becomes clear. The placing of people in space makes a plot point clearly and demonstrates where the power of the moment is and how it changes through the progression of the scene. The stage space has to be kept alive and animated, either by the placing of a person, or a chair, or object or a light, even where focus is concentrated on an intimate central moment. It is no good designing a beautiful scene that looks perfect in a maquette, only to find in the rehearsal room that live actors need to be exactly where the scenic elements have been planned. The maquette is not a theatre design exhibit with exquisitely made doll's house furniture and miniature people. Its sceno-graphic strength is to look unsatisfactory and incomplete until it is taken over and occupied by the performers on the stage, and becomes alive. All the different parts of the stage have to live at different times of the performance, through the use of light or the placing of the performers. Spaces that become unusable and locked off are dead spaces and can quickly make the staging seem heavy and dull. Actors need to be able to move through the many different parts of the stage in different shapes and configurations, fluently and naturally so that the audience's eye is constantly being taken from the extremities of the stage space to smaller focused moments. The direction or *mise en scène* clarifies and enhances the spoken or sung words.

The art of making theatre is transformative. No one knows before it starts where exactly a chosen direction will lead, since all the different disciplines involved have yet to make their contributions. Flexibility is required from the start, for if rigid ideas are introduced at this initial stage, creativity can be easily suffocated. The work between the director and the scenographer expands all the time, starting privately in a studio, and growing to the point where it has to be given away to the company to take it into another direction. As a company gets more and more confident, and becomes familiar with the material, they begin to be the authors of their own work, and to take possession of the project. The direction of a production is led and fashioned by a director, who must possess the conviction and enthusiasm necessary to lead the project through its various stages and have an overall technical knowledge and understanding. The director must also have vision and usually reputation, for it is this which is almost always the motivation for a production company's interest. A good director will be able to cast the right level of actors, and engage a like-minded team of creative and interpretative artists to carry out the work. The director will be greatly helped by the scenographer's knowledge of the text, its characters and context, an understanding of the performers and the ability to provide the research that supports the direction. Scenographers, architects of the dramatic space, are a part of the *mise en scène* – putting the staging into place, expressed through the colour and composition of the *écriture scénique* (the writing of the stage space – the visual image of the production).

Sadly, the ideal of collaboration is not always realised. The director and the scenographer often have a different perception of their relationship. A director will usually speak with admiration about a scenographer's contribution to the production, and how wonderful it is to work with a person so creative, amenable and flexible. It is perceived as happy, harmonious, and as intimate as any temporary union can be. However, when scenographers get together they reveal the opposite. From the way some directors talk, it is almost an affair of the heart; but these marriages made in heaven are often experienced by scenographers as marriages ending in hell. The talk amongst scenographers is of mistreatment, or being used as servants, in humiliating and ignoble ways. Often the work of the scenographer is publicly credited as being that of the director, who rarely contradicts this misconception. The same stories are told all over the world of scenographers feeling that their creative thinking, sometimes the motor of the work, is not properly recognised.

The responsibility for this situation does not lie with the director alone. Scenographers also have to look at their methods and expectations, and see where improvements can be made. Luciano Damiani, the Italian scenographer who has created many works with Giorgio Strehler in Italy and Roger Planchon in France, points out: "Different directors react differently to proposals, and often they find it hard to see what I see." Scenographers have to know when to yield, and when to be guided by aesthetic instinct. Directors need time to digest and to think when presented with drawings, sketches and ideas. What might be obvious to a trained visual artist is not always so clear to a director, and they have to become accustomed to "reading the drawing". Damiani also says:

> "Directors either give orders, insisting and demanding, or they want all the help and support they can get. Some know nothing – or not much and even seem colour blind and deaf. The job is to establish a common language, and to find this the scenographer has to really do the work if he wants to be taken seriously as a creative artist."[1]

As with any negotiated agreement, there has to be common ground from which to go forward. Like a director or an actor the scenographer is an interpreter of the text, and has to be flexible in approach until an agreed consensus is discovered. Directors have to understand that working with a scenographer is not like ordering goods for instant delivery. Scenography is highly labour intensive, and even with ever-improving technology is slow, often tedious. The scenographer is always juggling with textures, materials, proportions and relationships in order to discover a dramatic world that will work for the production. Trying out solutions in three-dimensional models simply takes time – days, sometimes weeks. To work with a director who can understand this is marvellous, but very few do. Picking up a cutting knife, ruler and card, or some paint and a pencil, and attempting to realise an idea manually and not just verbally can give the director some small idea of what is involved in the process, for it is likely that this was never experienced during education or training.

Closing these gaps in understanding starts with education. Because they are put on separate career paths directors and scenographers are polarised from the start. Normally directors enter the profession from university backgrounds, often through literature or drama and sometimes from subjects quite unrelated to theatre. Scenographers usually come

---

1   From the book by Giorgio Ursini Uršič, *Luciano Damiani: Architect de l'éphémère, Constructeur de théâtre*, Union des Théâtres de l'Europe, 1998.

through visual art schools. Even if they both come from university drama and theatre arts departments, or the many new performing arts courses, rigid course structures still exist, separating the different theatre arts and preventing mutual understanding. The least culpable are the art colleges, where making theatre performance pieces, installations, and video performance is part of the education. Art students can understand at first hand how it feels to perform, and how to direct others to do so. The same is not true for student actors and directors who only meet scenographers under the pressures of "in house" productions. Their experience is that designers are nothing more than a facility for providing instant sets, costumes and lights for the acting courses. Actors and directors should learn to draw, and scenographers should learn to act and direct, so that all could become totally literate and conversant with the multiple disciplines of the theatre. This would enable them to animate and exploit the stage space, to make productions vibrant in their staging as well as in their speaking.

Since the turn of the century the role of the director has changed from that of a stage organiser to a major artistic profession. By the mid-1950s, the job had developed into a profession where the director dominated the production, with other theatre workers playing a supporting role, much as film remains today. Directors were male, definitely authority figures, and were expected to get good performances from the cast. The cast in their turn usually vented all their frustration with the director on the designer by refusing to wear their costumes at the last moment. Staying up all night to remake costumes or to repaint the set overnight was quite normal, and many were the times I repainted a set with water, which made it look darker while the director was watching, only for it to dry out later and remain the same as it was originally. I quickly learned, as most designers do, the art of dissembling, and was taught when addressing a director never to say "*I* think" but always to precede it by asking "Do *you* think it would be a good idea to . . ." The tricks and deceptions were many, and, as I later discovered, universal. It seemed a foolish and futile way to behave. Actors too had their tricks. They came to rehearsals impeccably well groomed, with lipstick and polished nails, wearing hats and ties, addressing each other formally as Mr or Miss. They were expected to have learned their lines, and then would be told where to move by the director. They hardly noticed the design of "the background" for it was simply something they played *against* and not *with*. They always noticed their costumes. These were never referred to as clothes, which belonged only to the outside world. The final arbiter over any dispute was the director, who rarely took the side of the designer, being always too afraid to offend an actor or actress. Costumes were meant to reflect an actor's or actress's own personality, and not necessarily the character they were playing. Long discussions over the psychology of character and clothes were rare and frowned on. For the designers, it was a matter of being told this actress never wears green, or always likes long sleeves, or never wears anything with more than two colours. Designers were kept at a distance and expected not to interfere or be present at rehearsals, which were quite private affairs. The domain of the designer was The Workshop, usually a basement paint frame with an adjacent carpentry shop, and prop-making in a corner. Here was the kingdom of the theatre artisans, smelling of size glue, rancid paint and stale beer. This kingdom had its own language that only those with a registered right of entry understood. They often had their own system of measuring, and even made their own rulers that reconverted metric measurements back to imperial measures. Maquettes were no more than a guide to the finished product, for in those days part of the job was to adapt the design from stock scenery. The director never came to these areas, or knew anyone's names – nor was he very welcome. The Workshop never came to see the results of their work in performance. They had better things to do with any time off, and they mostly thought acting a peculiar activity and not a "proper job". The ladies in the Wardrobe, usually in cramped attics under the theatre roof, made costumes, cups of tea and dispensed theatre gossip. At the start of the technical week came the dreaded Dress Parade, where self-conscious actors and actresses would have to walk on the stage one by one, stand in the middle in a spotlight, and then take their place in a line up. The director, and possibly the producer and even the producer's wife, would sit mid-centre stalls and say what they thought of a costume. If they did not like it, they gave the order to have it remade or altered overnight. It was always a tense and humiliating experience for everyone. It convinced me that this was not the way I wanted to work.

This was the period of the famous World Theatre Seasons in London, which introduced the work of great European Directors, and the outstanding repertoire of national theatres presenting their own cultural heritage. The productions were performed in their own language, with neither subtitles nor surtitles. It marked the beginning of easier international travel and accessibility to international theatre through the growth of theatre festivals, which are now accepted as part of normal theatrical life. Being able to hear plays in their original language, to appreciate their sound, opened doors to the international language of theatre which communicates through in its production values, as well as its words. These productions that came to visit England from Europe brought with them a different kind of direction – that of the *mise en scène* in which the production was clearly attributed to the director, whose work was a new and original interpretation of well-known classic plays, or original creations from an ensemble theatre group that had been developing the work together over a long period of time. This concept of preparation time for a production emerged as the most significant difference between European-type theatre and its English and American counterparts, and relates to two completely different funding systems. In Great Britain, then as now, theatres are required to produce more productions in shorter preparation times each year, depending on the amount of their state subsidy. In Europe, directors led theatre companies and developed work with a company over a long period of time, only showing the results when they were deemed to be ready, and producing, as some still do, no more than two productions each year. This enabled the director and the scenographer to work and rework the ideas and to aim for and achieve productions of real quality that were ambassadors for the cultural policy of their country. Further-more, these productions testified to the re-emergence of the former stage decorator in a new creative role – as a scenographer working alongside the director, creating an iconography on the stage that visually summarised the intention and ethos of the production. It is significant that the rise of the European creative theatre director was almost always by reinvigorating classic plays by dead playwrights. In contrast, Great Britain, obliged to develop smaller productions, was witnessing another kind of creativity – the birth of a new playwriting period that also questioned the director's position. Some of the new writers became directors of their own plays, using only minimal scenic elements, in order to make sure it was the author's voice that was heard loud and clear and not a director's interpretation. Thus two completely different strands of theatre developed that, in retrospect, had much to give each other.

Both the European *mise en scène* and the British new plays movement shared a new directorial concept, which had profound effects for the scenographer. Up to this time plays were mostly written and staged in separate scenes, with a break in between each scene, usually done behind a front theatre curtain, or sometimes a special front cloth designed as part of the décor. The spectators entered the auditorium with the front curtain closed, and as the house lights went out, the curtain rose on a lit stage to reveal the scene. One of the lasting influences of these new productions was the introduction of one unified setting, which was visible to audiences as they came into the theatre. They could "come into the picture" as they took their seats, and merely a lighting change was sufficient to indicate the move from real time into dramatic time. Along with this was a new aim to find one visual metaphor or emblem that would serve as a unified setting for the whole play, rather than settings that required breaks between scenes for scene shifting. Dramatic changes of time or location within a unified setting could be made with the maximum of elegance and minimum of movement, by shifting the focus of the scene in the space rather than the scenery. Direction, choreography, music and light have become tools for creating cinematic scene changes, where performers cross the stage while furniture is being moved, in a series of small overlapping images, creating a seamless unity of direction and vision on the stage.

In 1969 the French director Roger Planchon, with the Théâtre Nationale Populaire from Villeurbanne, France, came to London to put on *Georges Dandin*, created with the scenographer René Allio. This was presented not as a comedy of manners but a human tragi-comedy, set in the real world of an affluent bourgeois farm typical of a large and recognisable section of provincial French society. The cuckolding of the yeoman farmer Georges Dandin, and his love and desire for Angélique, his duplicitous child bride from the town, was touching and heartbreaking. His eventual humiliation and downfall were played against the everyday life of the farm, where bread is baked, and farmhands make love in the hayloft, oblivious to the human tragedy happening in their midst. Planchon created two parallel worlds on the stage, portraying town and country, subtly interwoven at times, and yet seeming separate. René Allio, interpreting the direction, created a single stage picture of great beauty, enhanced with poetic light, that greatly added to the understanding of the play. Georges Dandin was set firmly in Molière's own time, the mid-seventeenth century. The actors were dressed in period clothes that looked lived in, yet could have almost been contemporary they were so well observed. The setting of the French farmhouse and outbuildings can be seen in rural France today, yet was completely in period and shown with such clarity that it was unnecessary to even think of transposing it to another time. Through these minute observations the spectators immediately entered the world of the play, a world of duplicity and intrigues in which this isolated farmhouse becomes a metaphor for French provincial society. Molière's stage direction of 1668 simply states "in front of Georges Dandin's house". Planchon and his company created a path for the production to travel that brought out and encouraged each of the various arts of the theatre: acting, painting, lighting, set dressing and prop-making. The *mise en scène* is validated when the direction, the use of space and light, and the scenography all speak with one voice and illuminate and enhance the text with new and fresh meaning.

I later had an opportunity to study several productions at the Théâtre Nationale Populaire, mostly written by Planchon, and to observe how they were made. This was my real theatre education in understanding the importance of the theatre director as the leader of the creation. Here I learned the relationship of text to action; how to create beauty on the stage, working from the smallest object to the largest. How nothing was good enough in its form and function if it did not also carry its own innate beauty and theatrical power. The productions were built up by creating many small evocative images within the scenes. These were worked on dramatically and visually, many being discarded, and eventually the remaining images linked together as entire scenes. The vision and text were totally integrated from the beginning of the work, and everyone was an essential part of the rehearsal process. I saw how to create an unseen world offstage indicated simply by the manner in which the actors arrived, sometimes running at speed with great urgency. Entrances and exits were incorporated into the first scenographic ideas, and many variations were explored. I have subsequently experimented with unusual ways of

THE ARRIVAL OF PERCY GIMLET IN A SHINY BLACK SEDAN CHAIR LIKE A ROLLS-ROYCE.

78   Figure 5.2   The arrival of Percy Gimlet, *John Brown's Body*

bringing the actors onto the stage – ways that indicate the world they have come from, such as the idea of combining an eighteenth-century sedan chair with a Rolls-Royce car to indicate the aristocratic world of Percy Gimlet in John McGrath's epic *John Brown's Body* (Figure 5.2). I saw how placing a well-chosen object could resonate with meaning and speak volumes. Each visual image in the play was tried out in many different ways, and assessed by the group of actors, technicians, assistant directors and scenographers, all of whom had a voice. During this period, Planchon was both author and director, and sometimes scenographer, supported by a dedicated team of interpreters. His thinking and requirements always came from a dogged search for the means to portray truth, often through comedy and "gags" both visual and verbal. He cared nothing for the theatrical practices of previous decades, but came to the theatre with a totally fresh and sometimes naïve eye.

A theatre director should be a cultural provocateur, as Joan Littlewood was in her Victorian Theatre Royal in the East End of London which she started in 1953 and headed for nearly twenty years. In this shabby and dilapidated building she created a rich theatre on meagre means, combining her love for work and play. She was dedicated to provide a public platform for the talent of all artists with a similar commitment to make a theatre that had a clear identity and purpose. At this time, in Great Britain, Joan Littlewood was unique, but it was not until twenty years later that women freelance directors started to make their presence known. Change was in the air. The Royal Shakespeare Theatre wanted to expand their touring policy and create a new production of *The Taming of the Shrew* with its own self-contained stage and seating. This was the ideal vehicle for two women in waiting – the director Di Trevis and myself – to create a new production. We seized the opportunity of the play within a play, to draw a picture of a company of poor itinerant actors, barely making a living trudging the length and breadth of the countryside yet transforming themselves into the fantastic characters in the play they were presenting entitled *The Taming of the Shrew – A Kind of History*. This play famously describes the well-known attitude of men towards women, but also, and perhaps more interestingly, demonstrates the worst aspects of the English obsession with class. It is considered amusing for a Lord to play a cruel joke on a person of the lower orders, poor, drunk and incapable. The prologue of the play begins with the appearance of a group of travelling players who have trudged wearily from their last venue, and have stopped for a rest outside the alehouse. They see poor Christopher Sly, ejected from the alehouse,   79 and are commissioned by the rich Lord of the manor to remove the drunk, take him to the Lord's house, and at the moment of his awakening perform their play for him, making him believe in his drunken stupor that he was in actual fact the Lord of the Manor. The Lord's page is commanded to dress up like a woman and pretend to be Sly's wife. For money and their survival, the actors agree to collaborate in the trick.

I was working on ideas for the production in a house facing the sea, watching people walking in slow procession along the narrow sea wall. A family returning from a picnic came into view. The women headed the procession, the first one pulling a battered pram by a bit of old string. It was being pushed by a heavily pregnant exhausted young girl carrying a baby. There was no room in the pram for the baby, for it was filled with picnic chairs, a table, various bits of old driftwood, toys and all the other paraphernalia of a family day out. Two more women followed, dragging small children. The children were all crying. This was a potent image that all mothers recognise. A short distance behind came the men, hands in pockets, smoking and laughing. They carried nothing, and seemed not to have a care in the world. They wore the oddest assortment of clothes: heavy boots, although it was dry, and duffel coats, although it was summer. They came so slowly into my view that I was able to draw them all quite easily, on a long thin piece of card I had quite by accident. (I love drawing on odd sizes of card – I never throw any away, and often it is the shape of the card itself that inspires me.) Later I showed this drawing (Figure 5.3) to Di Trevis, and, intrigued by the image, she proposed directing the production in a traverse staging that would allow the travelling players to arrive on

Figure 5.3   Drawing for *The Taming of the Shrew*

the stage, trudging like the family I had seen, exhausted and weary. She thought this would be an opportunity to show that the women travelling players were both actresses in the company and wives and mothers in ordinary life. The young women actresses would have stage characters when performing *The Taming of the Shrew* but would still have to pack up and clean the floor at the end. The pram would carry all the props and scenery. The men would be tunelessly whistling "Where is the life that late I led?" – the song of the show. The lot of both Sly and the women was not after all so different. From this one drawing came a non-stop flow of ideas and suggestions. I raided markets and antique dealers, buying bits of old clothing, often so rotten that they were of no use to anyone for very little money. I cut them up and remounted them on to corsets and underwear, so that the costumes for the play within a play were suggested and ragged, and not in any way complete. I made skirts out of discarded nineteenth-century bed quilts that evoked a memory of Elizabethan costume. The "école de rag-bag" style was both authentically "period" and very modern, and captured the jumble-sale quality of the family I had observed by the sea. At one performance I heard a spectator observe that the poor actors must have got paid in old clothes from all the houses they had visited, instead of money; that remark was exactly right! A playing area was created twenty-five metres long by six metres wide, with banks of stadium seating either side. It could easily be erected in the sports halls and leisure centres that were the venues on the tour. Entrances for the actors and public were made possible at either end, with two breaks in the middle of the seating block. A black wooden floor ran the length of the playing area, and above

it was a white silk retractable ceiling pulled on wires by stage management hidden behind small vertical walls at either end. An interior was simply created by pulling the silk ceiling very fast from one end of the playing space to the other. The travelling players piled up all the Lord of the Manor's furniture at one end of the polished black floor, and threw an old backcloth over it that said "The Taming of the Shrew – A Kind of History", as indeed it was. They took their shoes off and marked a chalk circle on the floor in which they presented to the drugged and drunken Sly this story of profane love. Shakespeare writes a prologue for Sly, but there is no epilogue. We added a silent epilogue, where the girl who has just played Kate has to clear up after all the actors, and wash the floor. Sly watches her. She throws him a coin that has been tossed to the actors for payment. They are both in the same economic boat. This was an example of director and scenographer working collaboratively within their own area of expertise; one with the space, actors and costume, and one in the space with actors and text to tell the story. Both worked from the same starting point – a drawing from real life.

A scenographer's relationship to the director can be complex and fragile. The production needs to be set up from the beginning on a time-scale that allows debate, compromise and persuasion. If scenographer and director can begin with a clean slate, isolating the problems rather than seeking instant solutions, there is a real possibility of working together in a partnership of trust. Too often either the designer expects to be told by the director what to do, and then does various versions to "get it right", or the director expects the designer to come up with the solution which will be the peg on which to hang the entire production. In order to achieve a creative harmony both need to have the honesty to begin their work on an equal basis. Above all they need to invest time in the preparation of the project to evolve a method of staging and an individual language for the play. Without time to explore and make mistakes, decisions right or wrong have to be made, and solutions have to be bought in at any cost. There is no room for chance, and accident. The painter Robert Rauschenberg says "for me, art shouldn't be a fixed idea that I have before making it. I want to include all the fragility and doubt that I go through the day with . . . I like to go into the studio not having any ideas. I want the insecurity of not knowing – like performers feel before a performance."[2] This fragility is

2   *New York Times*, © 2000.

Figure 5.4a Rehearsal drawing, *The Cherry Orchard*

central to a theatre production which is always balanced on the abyss of the unknown. Performances say the same words, but are different every night – full of chance and the possibility that things may go wrong. This is the thrill and tension of live performance. It is up to the scenographer, as a first-hand inventor, to lead the vision in the right direction, and not expect to be told what to do. On the other hand, the scenographer should not be expected to guess what is in the director's mind without being told. This is precisely why quick unselfconscious drawings, that are another way of

Figure 5.4b Rehearsal drawing, *The Cherry Orchard*

Figure 5.4c Rehearsal drawing, *The Cherry Orchard*

speaking, are so valuable, and give reality to a director's thoughts and a concrete image for both director and scenographer so that both can travel in the same direction (see Figures 5.4a, b, c, d). The scenographer has to be able to guide the director's eyes to using what is given to the best advantage. The most difficult thing to overcome is a director who does not know or cannot see how to use the ideas that have been agreed upon. When a director wants to exploit the theatre for what it can uniquely provide, creation is born. With an empty space and an actor the greatest feats of the imagination are possible. I once said: "A scene at the top of the Eiffel Tower? Buy me a souvenir model three inches high, place it in a stage light, and get the actor to look down. A fire? Simple. Let the actor strike a match in the darkness, and another run and scream." Only a good understanding between director and scenographer can achieve cool and easy magic that costs nothing but is so powerful and exists only on a stage.

The external image of a theatre should project the artistic and political attitude of its director, so that each theatre "house" has its own special identity. Opening doors for guest directors and visiting productions is all part of the philosophy, and a commitment to extend the loyal audience's theatrical experience. Theatre needs to be directed by a person of vision and commitment, supported by an equally gifted and committed administrator, plus a small team of multi-talented artists whose remit is quite simply to do really good work. No matter how clever a business plan, or

Figure 5.4d Rehearsal drawing, *The Cherry Orchard*

how efficient the marketing department may be, unless the work is good there is absolutely no point in running a theatre. A theatre director can have an important influence in creating the cultural climate of a community and the organisation of theatre.

Theatre-making has been cited by business leaders as an example of good practice and demonstrates how independence and togetherness can be productively combined. The prime motivator is the production, and its values are put before profit. The influential thinker and writer on business and work ethics, Charles Handey, states: "There is nothing more exciting than losing oneself in a cause that is bigger than oneself, something that makes self-denial worthwhile, where pride in the work and passion for its purpose are the driving forces and where success is shared, not hugged to oneself in secret."[3] This is the most precise description of the shared experience the director and the scenographer aim to achieve.

---

3 Discussion, "Business in the Arts", organised by Julia Rowntree of the London International Festival of Theatre and held at Three Mills Island, Bromley by Bow, July 1999.

CHAPTER 6

PERFORMERS The Scenographic Actor

Since scenographers take on responsibility for creating the total stage look – scenic elements, costumes, props, and furniture – each individual has to decide where their own areas of interest and priorities fall. I declare my increasing interest to be in working collaboratively with a director to realise the full potential of the actor in the space.

The human being is at the centre of live theatre, and both the director and the scenographer start working from the actor – the most powerful living element in the space. Just as a director's first task is to release good performances from the actors in order to tell the story of the play, so the scenographer brings specific visual skills and knowledge to the production. A play can happen without scenery, but there is always at least one performer to be considered, and that performer has to wear something. Costumes therefore become the extension of the actor in space. They create an entire world enhanced by light, that can be understood without any scenery at all. When designers redefine themselves as scenographers, they signify that they are willing to go further than just designing sets and costumes to create an attractive stage picture. It means they are prepared to watch and study the actors in rehearsal, understand how a performance grows, and how the stage environment and the costumes can work together to enhance the actor's performance. It is not always easy. Actors are mobile, unpredictable, possessing a transforming power onstage, different every night, and dangerous. It is the scenographer's job to find how to communicate with the actors, evaluate their needs and wishes, and make the right decisions that will achieve a united and harmonious result.

A scenographer has to earn, develop and maintain the trust of the performers, who, night after night, have to go out onto the empty dark stage, and with total confidence recreate the vision for a half-seen audience. There are two principal aspects: working with the performer to help him or her create the role, and working with the director to help place the performer dynamically and actively in the stage space. The performer should be encouraged not just to wear a costume, be it period or modern, but to inhabit it, turning it from a costume into a second skin. Through studying and understanding the human body, the space it occupies and displaces, the director and scenographer can model and sculpt the stage eloquently and dramatically with the performers.

At the beginning of a new project, many of the cast and production team will be strangers to each other until they meet on the first day of rehearsal to begin a new adventure together. This is the beginning of an intense period of work, where everyone very quickly gets to know each other, becomes aware of abilities and uncertainties, until, miraculously, a production is born. However, no sooner is the production on then it is over, and what has seemed so important evaporates, and the whole process starts again with a new set of people. All that remains is the memory of the experience, some photographs and reviews. After the production is

Figure 6.1   Life studies of Albie Woodington in *King Henry IV*

over, the drawings and costume designs, the concrete remnants of the production, acquire a different value. Conceived as working drawings, they become the production record – evidence for historians and researchers and a growing number of art collectors. There is a fascination with costume drawings; they are not only pictures in their own right, but also show how actors can be totally transformed into other characters through the colour, form and texture of the costumes (Figure 6.1).

I try not to do elaborate costume drawings before the rehearsals begin, and the whole company have met each other, although I do carefully research the period and bring to the first day of rehearsals as much background material as the costume interpreter and I have been able to collect. I always want to leave a space for the actors' contributions, which only start to become clear after a few days of work together. However, actors do need a guiding eye, for they are not always the best judge of what they should wear on stage or indeed in real life! Often ideas come while watching the actors work in rehearsal, and new and unthought of possibilities suddenly become clear. This is exactly the time that the closest liaison is needed between director, scenographer and actors so that the play can be modelled,

Figure 6.2a Rehearsal sketch, *The Cherry Orchard*

shaped and reshaped. Being present at as many rehearsals as possible, draw-ing what is happening, and working alongside the director is absolutely essential for any meaningful discussion about the intention of the scene and the needs of the actors. There is a great difference between theoretical ideas and what actually happens in practice (Figure 6.2).

Actors communicate to a designer through an emotional vocabulary, and establishing common ground for a dialogue takes time and patience on

Figure 6.2b Rehearsal sketch, *The Cherry Orchard*

both sides. There is an actors' language used to describe the issues that affect their performance, often closely connected with their costumes, props and furniture. It both masks and reveals hopes, anxieties and vulnerability, and is expressed as "feeling": "I *feel* the train of this dress is too long for the character I am playing"; "I *feel* the length of these sleeves could be longer"; "I *feel* this chair could be bigger/smaller/lower/higher"; "I *feel* this door is in the wrong place." Few actors have a visual vocabulary – usually through no fault of their own. Drama schools and courses rarely teach this, and even young actors refer to "costume girls" and "props girls" without realising how offensive this can be. Good communication with actors starts by being able to listen very carefully to often-hesitant language, and to interpret it correctly. The scenographer needs to have both an authority and flexibility, and to have the total support of the director from the start so that actors become familiar with the language of visual imagery that links with the text, and may give a new perspective to the work.

The scenographer cannot expect to gain the actor's confidence without being familiar with the text, its dramatic structure, characters, plots and subplots, and there is no substitute for proper preparatory work. In those suspended hours in the rehearsal room, reality ceases to be the trials and tribulations of everyday life but is instead the dilemmas and conflicts of the world of the play that is being created. Everybody concerned with the production has to get to know the fictional characters and their world and join in imagining how they lived and survived in the period of the play. A knowledge of history helps to put this work into context for the actors, especially if it can be illustrated by pictorial references and artefacts in a Living Museum that is a resource for everyone to use. It is extremely helpful to this important process to be in the rehearsals as much as possible, and this depends on having a good supportive technical team, who can be visiting the scenic and costume workshops while I am observing and recording the rehearsal images as they are created. These visual notes become the actual storyboard of the production, and enable all the fast-moving rehearsal information to be absorbed at first-hand and quickly acted upon. Instead of discovering that scenic elements, or furniture, are the wrong size at a stage when nothing can be altered, modifications can be built in as part of the ongoing process; this usually proves to be both artistically and financially beneficial.

❖

There are nine small drawings by Veronese for *Oedipus Tyrannus* hidden in a dark corner of the Getty Museum in Los Angeles. They are drawings of contemporary clothes for a theatre production, and are possibly the first costume designs recorded on paper. Drawn quickly and unpretentiously, Paolo Veronese's natural ability leads him to place the figures in expressive poses on the paper. They are clearly observations from everyday life, people in clothes, but transported by Veronese's red chalk to the ancient Greek world of myth and mystery. They are working drawings, nine figures crammed together with notes and scribbles explaining what is needed. Although they are small, they appear large and vibrant, bursting out of the frame of the paper. With a healthy disrespect for posterity they have been folded into four, no doubt stuffed in a pocket. They are works of art, yet are contemporary clothes seen in the everyday world of the Verona of the mid-1500s.

Costume, however, is not confined to the realistic portrayal of everyday clothes, for as in ancient times the combination of symbolic colour, texture and tradition conveys a secret dialogue to the spectator. Ease of travel, and the ability to see traditional arts all over the world, plus the information highway, has created an accessible cultural pool of ideas from Japan, China, India and Africa, that western countries have plundered in their never-ending search for new inspirations. Ariane Mnouchkine's production of *Les Atrides*, created with the scenographer Guy-Claude François at the Cartoucherie in Paris, brilliantly used this cross-cultural opportunity, combining influences from East and West. Actors' faces are painted like masks, their mouths and eyes heavily accented and coloured. Their expression comes from their gestures and physical body movements, as well as from their stylised voices. The bare arena in which they perform forces the audience to become aware of the extraordinary shapes of these actors both singly and as a whole group, silhouetted against the harsh ochre stone walls. In a second a scene turns from vibrant aggression to tragedy by simply changing the costumes from red to black. The use of a group of performers as a chorus of comment or dissent, occupying the arena and confronting the audience, is a device as powerful today as it was in the ancient Greek theatre, and is often used in opera. It gives the visual artist an opportunity to build a bold picture on stage in colour and shape, and then to dramatically change the image by deconstructing or splitting the group into individual images that form a totally different composition on the stage. The chorus becomes a scenographic device for changing the mood and atmosphere of the scenes, swiftly using the colour of the costumes seen *en bloc* to describe the passing of time and dramatic events. A group, or chorus directly addressing the audience, is a powerful tool.

Figure 6.3   Chorus drawing for *Happy Birthday Brecht*

When the chorus works together, changing its physical shape from within, it takes on the value of a plastic and mobile scenic element (Figure 6.3).

The body is the structure on which the scenographer creates and builds costumes, and the constant practice of life drawing is the anchor for artists to develop an anatomical understanding that underpins costume creation. Each part of the body has a cause and effect upon another part, which in turn speaks of the way the body has experienced its life. The displacement of weight in the body and the thrust of the head through the spine convey age, occupation and status. Constrictions of corsets and underclothes, heights of shoes, and weights of wigs and hairstyles further affect the body's posture. As well as formal life study, historical portraits, paintings and photographs are a primary source of reference for reinterpretation, as are personal notes and sketches observed from daily life (Figure 6.4). Costume is the artistic medium that describes class, history, and personality. It can also create the whole scenic atmosphere, and is a direct and immediate way of working with performers.

AGNES IN THE MORNING : JULIA FORD
SCHOOL FOR WIVES.

Figure 6.4 Drawing of Samantha Cones as model for Julia Ford's Agnès in *The School for Wives*

The language of clothes and materials reveals country, class, age and taste. The ability to isolate these characterics sets the scene of the play, and gives the actor cues to building and sustaining a suggestion that through the progress of the play becomes a fact. It gives the audience the thoughts of the actor, the director, and the words of the text, in the most concrete terms. Colour can take on different meanings and implications according to the character in the play, and the ability of the actor to use the costume creatively. An example is to consider how different the colour black can be when shown in different contexts (Figure 6.5). In Act 3 of *Hedda Gabler*, Hedda comes in dressed in black. There is something defiant about this black. The audience senses that it is not a mark of respect for the death of her husband's elderly aunt, a person Hedda hardly knew or cared about. Where did Hedda acquire this dress? Did she have it made at vast expense on her six-month honeymoon journey with her husband that so tortured her, and did it cost more money than she could possibly afford? Perhaps it was the dress she wore at the funeral of her father, the late General Gabler, and she had it brought from her own home before she went on her honeymoon, knowing it would be waiting for her on her return. Her dress enfolds her like a shroud. She is in denial of her own life, and as in Greek tragedy this is a signal pointing to her own imminent death. It is a mysterious dress, that, like all good scenic images, implies more than it shows. In Ibsen's play *The Masterbuilder*, Solness's wife Aline is similarly dressed in black, but this is a different black. It is the black of guilt and punishment. She is in mourning for her nine lost dolls, and her two children. She receives no warmth or emotional support from her husband. Her black dress must be severe, restricting, modest, suggesting that she has worn it every day for the past nine years since the burning down of her parents' house changed her life.

Masha in Chekhov's *The Seagull* also wears black. Unhappily married to the local schoolteacher, and without her own identity, she has lost interest in her appearance, although she is clearly an attractive woman. She says she is in mourning for her life. Her version of black is workmanlike, practical, thin and narrow, possibly home-made and in direct contrast to her own personality which shines through in contradiction to her outer black shell. Black costumes are never neutral. They make very strong statements about attitude, and states of mind, as in the reproachful black clad women in Federico García Lorca's *House of Bernarda Alba*, where the green dress specified for Adela is like a wild bird's cry for liberation from her caged existence.

However brilliant the costume drawing, the fitting room is where the real creative costume work begins, whether the costume is made new or recreated from the rows of lifeless used costumes in a hire store and brought back to life again. The drawing is only the guide. The real work of costume creation is a joint effort of scenographer, performer and makers working together, looking directly at an actor in the fitting-room mirror so everyone involved can see the cut, line, and construction as well as the colour combinations. The scenographer has to be able to draw with scissors on the material draped on a costume stand or live actor, to understand the line of

ALINE BASIC BLACK

MASHA ACT 2
FINE BLACK CARDIGAN
(OVER SKA)
OLD BLACK

HEDDA BLACK
PLEATED SILK & VELVET

Figure 6.5   Three women in black: drawings of Masha, Aline and Hedda

95

a period, and to know how to adapt it to the proportions of a performer. It is essential to start with the right period underwear and corsets that give the body a structure, and to provide correct shoes that dictate the posture of the actor. Then, a plain calico toile, the basic pattern interpreted from the drawing, can be fitted over the underwear. The actor needs to have corsets, shoes, and long practice skirts in rehearsal so that they can get used to the weight and stance dictated by the clothes. The scenographer and the costume maker can work quickly and directly onto the body of the performer to perfect or alter the line and cut, sculpting the material to the proportions of the actor, before cutting into the actual fabric. A good visual memory and knowledge of period line and shape is invaluable, so that the essence is preserved while at the same time creating something individual and appropriate to the vision of the production. These work sessions in a fitting room are the most intimate moments between a performer and a scenographer, and ones in which trust and confidence are essential. They must not be tense or rushed, and actors should go back to the rehearsal room feeling confident and happy, and with a clear picture of how they will look firmly imprinted in their memory. The fitting room work is an extension of the actors' work on the text. As the character of the play appears in the fitting room mirror, everyone can start to imagine what that person would have worn as ornament or jewellery, and all the other details that personalise clothes.

Naturally, performers feel extremely vulnerable when they are looking at their near-naked selves in a harshly lit mirror. All performers are acutely conscious of their worst physical defects. The costume, though, can compensate for these real or imagined deficiencies. Tact and psychology, coupled with an understanding of the character to be played, have to be the languages of the fitting room, with a quiet and authoritative calm estab-lished. The skill of the costume-maker in cutting and manipulating the material can usually avert a crisis. I always listen carefully to how actors talk about themselves and their needs because this shows me that they know and understand their own physique and tastes. All this helps the costume. When an actor is willing to co-operate in the making of a costume the result is more successful than when someone stands like a mannequin in front of the mirror with arms outstretched saying "transform me". The actor also must be sensitive to the costume-maker, whose work also comes under scrutiny and who can feel very vulnerable. Costume-maker are artists and have to be given time to create from flat fabric a round structure on a body, and to be guided to exaggerate or subtly alter a line to fit a specific actor. The costume drawing is a mark of respect for the artistry of the costume maker as much as it is for the actor, and should leave enough room in its interpretation for the individuality of the maker to contribute to the finished item. A set of costumes on a rail ready to be delivered is as exciting as a new collection of fashion clothes, for they are just waiting to be worn. The actors imprint is already built into the seams, decoration and fabric.

The choice of fabrics is crucial to the interpretation of a costume design. Feeling samples of the fabric enables actors to think how they could use the costume dramatically. Just as in ordinary life, it is pleasant to wear good clothes made out of sympathetic materials. If a fabric is wrongly "cast" at this decision-making stage, it will never be right for the part. No amount of work will make a fabric behave in a manner of which it is incapable. Each fabric must be assessed for its weight, hang, durability, relationship to the drawing, suitability for the character, period potentiality, ability to be enhanced with dye or paint, and its relationship in texture to other materials on the stage – and easy maintenance.

The Korean scenographer Lee Byong-Boc has understood profoundly the power of the costumed actor in the empty space, and has used this belief to illuminate interpretations from the world repertoire of plays in Europe and at home. In order to develop her theories further she and her husband, the painter Kwon Ok-Yon, have restored and rebuilt, stone by stone, an ancient palace in the Korean countryside called "*total-musée*". Here on a rectangular lake with a floating platform stage is an open-air theatre, totally at one with nature, a key element in Korean culture. Three sides of the lake are backed by low temple buildings, also used as dressing rooms for the actors. The curved roofs of the building are painted and decorated with wooden flowers to reproduce the shape of the undulating Korean Hills in which "*total-musée*" is situated. The performance space it embraces is at once expectant and frightening. Two hundred people can sit in the natural auditorium on low wooden benches placed on the "fourth wall" of the rectangle. From the painted temples, the shadows of the actors can be seen in hidden courtyards, making their preparations and creating a sense of anticipation that something is shortly going to happen.

The actors' entrance is masked by a wall of bright garish posters. A modern female shaman and her troupe of actors, all relatives, emerge larger than life, to tell a traditional morality tale of myth and mysticism, fear and power. They wear a contemporary version of traditional costumes, made in Lee Byong-Boc's favourite materials of straw, hessian, plants, and earth overlaid with translucent lengths of brilliantly coloured silk organza. The actors, however, have added their own touches. They have added an incongruous assortment of sneakers, trilby hats, acrylic socks, and some smoke pipes and cigarettes as they sit watching the action from the side of the stage. From the first appearance of the shaman, there is no question who has the power. Before giving us a word of the story, she produces an enormous butterfly net on a pole, which she extends into the audience and passes round without stepping off the stage. We are instructed to put money in it, otherwise the story will bring us bad luck; of course we obey. This is repeated several times during the evening, just as the tension seems to mount. She takes her time and counts the money on stage to see if enough has been collected to allow her to continue, and she asks the opinion of her cast. Bit by bit, with more and more daring, the tale is told. We do whatever we are asked, including going onto the stage to join in a dance we have no idea how to perform – even the most reticent amongst us join in. And all the time she is both in the character, and a cunning business woman. We see her guile and cunning as she manipulates her audience to the maximum, and when the performance has finished the day's work is done. She counts her money and goes, oblivious of the audience who have been totally seduced. Lee Byong-Boc says, "Theatre is nothing other than the dramatic images and stories that fill the vacuity of an empty space with the presence of the costumed actor."

Samuel Beckett's plays also fill an empty space with the presence of an actor. In *Not I* a very complicated technical structure, that supports a standing actress several feet above the stage floor, appears to the audience like a black void in which only a moving mouth is visible, seemingly suspended in space. The actor and the scenographer have to work in close co-operation to achieve this, for, if the illusion is not perfect, the piece will be destroyed. It hangs on a delicate balance. In *Krapp's Last Tape* one solitary actor, in an empty space with the debris of his life unseen in a half-open drawer, has to convey his whole world past and present. Although there appears to be nothing on the stage, there is a huge amount of work to achieve that nothingness and to find the right table and chair, and objects for the actor that are both practical and poetic. There is so much unseen work between an actor and a scenographer. Samuel Beckett knew this clearly in his detailed technical description of the requirements for Winnie in *Happy Days*. This is a text in which the author gives so many instructions, and in fact provides the calico toile of the production that at first it seems that every production must simply be a replica of a previous

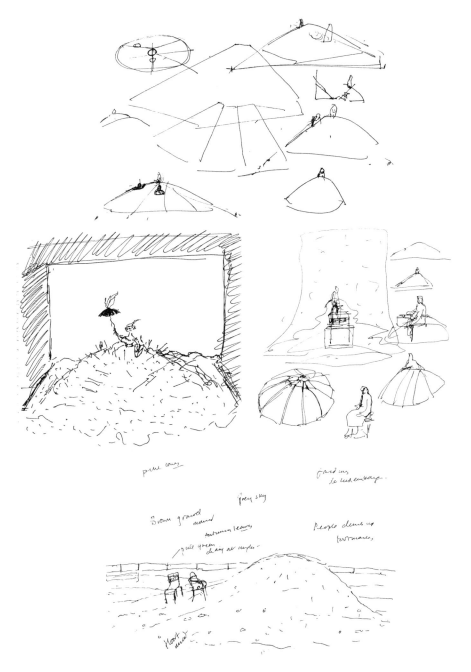

Figure 6.6   Early sketches for *Happy Days*

one. But every Winnie brings a completely different story. Her speech, inflection, and the choice of objects in her bag that she sets on top of her mound, like a Chardin still-life painting, show that once there is a solid structure to the piece the imagination can fly. Winnie's costume is only seen from the waist upwards, and from those details, her hat, her bag with personal contents, the audience can imagine her former life "in the old style". What the audience do not see is how she is able to sit in the mound without moving. She has first to be strapped securely into a chair with good back support on a platform. This platform has to be calculated so that her seated figure makes her high enough to hide her husband, Willy, who lives unseen at the back of the mound (Figure 6.6). Failure to do this will ruin Winnie's line, and also the laugh when Willy's hand suddenly appears from behind to hand her the medicine bottle she has just thrown over. What is not seen is the complicated substructure of the mound. She has to get in it, so it has to have a concealed opening. It also gets very, very hot in such an enclosed space, so an electric cooling fan is used, necessitating thick foam soundproofing inside the surface of the mound. She needs a footrest to help support her. There has to be discreet padding, first around her waist and then around her neck when she appears to sink further into the mound. As a neck is smaller than a waist, an extra piece has to be added that matches exactly the rest of the mound. She must be physically comfortable and relaxed, for playing Winnie is a huge feat of memory for any actress. The work demands careful and patient trial and adjustment between actor and scenographer before anything else can begin, following exactly Beckett's instruction, for, of course, he cunningly worked it all out.

A stage is an empty space that is filled bit by bit, and emptied again in ever-changing patterns created by the movement of actors through the scene. Actors often have a very good instinctive sense of where they should be, and how they can use the space effectively. In planning a production at the Swan Theatre in Stratford-on-Avon, a small open stage surrounded by the audience on three sides, we had to create the belief that the play was taking place in a huge country house. The only way we could do this was by describing the unseen house through the actions of the actors. Dancing couples burst onto the stage as if the dance had begun in another room and had spread all over the mansion (Figure 6.7). They filled the stage with their energy and colour; as they danced off one solitary figure was left to take command of the following contrasting still scene. Directors and actors often use furniture imaginatively, inventing different angles and positions

Figure 6.7   Swan Theatre, early drawings of Elgar's "Rondo"

to sit on chairs and at tables. Watching this evolve, the scenographer can also adjust the proportions and heights so that it helps and accentuates the playing – as Caspar Neher used to do. Neher invented his own form of measurement for tables and chairs that became known as "neher-height" to his colleagues. He used to have the furniture cut down by five or ten centimetres below normal, so that the audience could see the top surfaces of the tables, and the actors would not sit just anyhow, but would have to adopt specific attitudes and gestures. Neher's many drawings show how an actor's body could be elongated on a chair, how to sit at an angle on a chair which is itself placed at an angle to a table, and how to create rooms and compositions just through the placing of some chairs – as long as it all helps the playing. Chairs have to be chosen very carefully and have the advantage of being very mobile and portable, each one with its own character. They become like extra actors in the space, helping to make scene changes a series of fluid overlapping images that do not stop the action of the play.

The form of staging a play – in a proscenium, round, end, traverse or promenade – affects both the spectator and performer. Each form has its own dynamic to be understood and exploited. When performers are surrounded on more than one side by the spectators, their view must not be obscured by scenery or large pieces of furniture, yet they must have what is needed to play the scene. The actors acquire an enhanced prominence, and their inner thoughts and reactions clearly register, not just through their eyes, but also through the use of their bodies in three dimensions. The actors assume a huge power, and if they do it with enough conviction they can make the audience believe whatever they choose. It is often unwise to try and define in advance how an actor should play a scene, but rather leave space, and see how to capitalise on the performer's inventiveness and instinctive use of the space. This is how Opera Transatlántica, a group of international theatre and visual artists, works. The company holds several exploratory workshops prior to a full production, exploring the interaction of performer, object, space and text. The actors are given several themes to work on, and a scenario of the structure of the scenes with a skeleton dialogue that will be later developed into a complete script. In the rehearsal room there is an assortment of simple objects – small chairs, a rope and some walking sticks, and some basic art materials for constructing anything that might be missing and needed. Much thought is given to finding sources of free materials for costumes and props, such as a collection of old unwanted tablecloths ranging from elaborate lace and damask confections to modern bright-coloured plastic. Opera Transatlántica aims to find a theatrical way of moving swiftly through time and place to create "journey plays" that tell stories of cultural identity, and how people move from place to place through history and time. Simple real objects are used in unexpected ways depending entirely on the actor's inventiveness and ability to make imaginative transformations before the audience's eyes. One day, working on a scene that takes place in a small town square surrounded by small "houses", we witnessed how powerful this can be. The scene was set in a small town in Venezuela sometime in the twentieth century. It is night, dark and quiet, and four gaily coloured front doors are firmly closed. Three drunken soldiers who have just lost their jobs arrive looking for someone to blame. They start to hurl abuse at the householders, throw beer at the doors and before very long the quiet scene turns into an ugly riot. Eventually the soldiers lose interest and depart, leaving a frightening atmosphere in the air. Cautiously the housewives open the doors and warily emerge to see if it is safe. We had no desire or ability to construct houses, or even front doors, as the aim was to maintain fluency between the scenes. Suddenly one of the actors folded a bright tablecloth into a long rectangle and held it up in front of her to obscure her figure entirely. Her stillness made the tablecloth into a solid wooden door. Then she slowly lowered it a little bit and peered round the side, gradually "opening" the door. It was a most beautiful discovery, especially when all four "doors" did the same. Such simple actions show how good acting can be more telling than expensive effects. When they thought it was safe to come out, they carefully wiped the "doors" clean, and folded them away, and went into the next scene. In a subsequent scene the story took place in three different houses visited in quick succession by an elderly salesman and his younger companion. Two small sturdy pink and blue chairs were placed in the middle of the acting space. They looked as if they were having a conversation with each other across the empty space. We discovered when the scene was played in front of one chair, it became an interior of a house, and when the scene was reversed and played in the opposite direction with the other chair, it became the neighbour's house. When two people sat in both chairs and talked to each other shoulder to shoulder, they appeared to be in yet another house. These scenographic discoveries were made by the actors themselves working with the actual objects, and conveying a belief to the audience that two small chairs could stand for a whole neighbourhood. Two small chairs, four tablecloths and some brave and imaginative actors were all that was needed to paint a picture of a small town, and create a rich theatre out of little means that could be one way forward to redis-covering what drama is actually about, and how actors and artists can make memorable creations together.

CHAPTER 7

SPECTATORS The Great Mystery

The scenographer's work is not complete until the first audience arrives in the theatre and the moment comes to make the weeks of private preparation, public. Sitting amongst the audience, the director and the scenographer can see if the peice which seemed so clear in the privacy of the rehearsal room can be clearly understood. The process of making theatre is only complete when the spectators become part of the event, and a new phase of the work begins as the production moves from the subjective to the objective. How the ideas of text, research, colour and composition, direction and performers actually work is now judged by the spectators' eyes and ears. By sitting in the audience, at performances, the whole integrated production can be viewed critically and differently each time, comparing the reactions of one group of spectators with another. Was the intention of each moment made clear? Did the idea have the supposed emotional response? Was the audience taken into the created world of the play? Could it all have been placed and composed better?

When the play is up and running I like to study as many performances as possible, and just as in dress rehearsals on stage, sit in a different part of the house every night so that I can really test whether theories work in practice. Once the preview period is over it is very difficult to make modifications, but change is not my objective. This is primarily self-education, and I take notes and make drawings to store up and apply to the next piece of work. I certainly learn more from audiences than from any other source, not only by looking at my own work but also by seeing other productions as part of the audience.

There is a paucity of good debate about the work. Months of sincere effort are often passed off with just a few casual remarks; but informed discussion is what most people long for. Critics have their own specialisms and, although they officially review a production, rarely include any acknowledgement of its wider context, although they often compare the past to the present. They feel that they have to concentrate primarily on the literary or narrative theme, explaining the plot to the readers as the potential audience. It is not surprising that the visual aspect may only get a brief mention or comment, and the look of a production may well be credited entirely to the director. There is a scenic vocabulary that speaks of the use of space, planes and diagonals, and colour. It is little used by drama critics. Their written descriptions have to be able to reflect their critical views, and also encourage readers to buy the paper, and hopefully a ticket. There is not much to be learned from these small printed columns. If a scenographer wants real critical feedback that is honest and useful, fresh and unbiased, then that is to be found sitting objectively and anonymously in an auditorium with an audience, studying their reactions, and overhearing their critical comments and conversations.

In large capital cities and commercial theatres it is difficult to have any direct encounter with audiences beyond judging the effect from the length of the applause at the end. Touring plays offer a unique opportunity to be guests in a town, and, through open-house, post-play discussions, to meet directly with the audiences. This builds a loyalty that will encourage audiences to keep coming back to see other productions once they have become familiar with the ethos of the company. This educative work with an audience has benefits both ways. The audiences can see productions without having to travel to a capital city, and the theatre company can get direct feedback and be able to evaluate how the production has been received, and use this information when planning future tours. An education and outreach programme that is integrated into the work of the theatre company, with all members of the company committed to participate in group or individual skills sessions and talks, is an important way to attract new and young audiences to discover an enjoyable group activity. It used to be thought that 'the magic of the theatre' would be ruined if its secrets were revealed to the audience. Quite the opposite is true. Audiences are curious and enthralled to be let in behind the scenes, to be shown how a play is visualised, and see the maquettes and the drawings. They are fascinated by the process, and this greatly influences how they receive the work. They will already have a sense of involvement and understanding. When the actors, director and scenographer meet the audience in post-show discussions, the audience sees the actors that have just left the stage in character and costume re-appear some moments later as ordinary people, in their street clothes, tired but happy to listen. Suddenly the roles are reversed, for this time it is the audience who must perform for the company and ask questions about the production.

One night at a post-show discussion of Ibsen's *The Masterbuilder* produced by English Touring Theatre, a young 'A' level Theatre Studies student stood up. Hesitantly and self-consciously he began his question by stating "I am only interested in physical theatre, and I have only ever seen physical theatre, and I only came to see this because it is on my 'A' level Theatre Studies syllabus. But when I saw that young girl come in through the door with all the light coming in behind her, I said to myself, here's trouble – and then when I saw Solness's wife come in, I thought well, I can't blame him because she's so miserable and who would want to live with someone like that. And then when I found out that they had started their married lives living in her parent's house that had burned down, and their babies had died, I thought well, I can't blame her for being miserable, because they never really had a chance . . ." He then went on without pausing for breath to summarise the whole plot of the play, finishing with "and so I only really like physical theatre, but I thought this was great". He received a standing ovation for his performance from both us on the stage and the rest of the audience.

The audience, for which all the effort of months of work has been made, remains a mystery – a group of disparate people who have all decided to do the same thing on the same night, and come together in a large space called a theatre. When they arrive they are all separate strangers, but within seconds they become a community – a group of people who actors quickly describe as "good" or "bad", "a bit sluggish tonight" or "rather stuffy" or "really quick and brilliant". This gives this abstract concept a name and an identity of which the audience is unaware. There is a point in the rehearsal process when actors can do no more with the material, until they can play it in front of the missing ingredient – the audience. There is no fail-safe formula of how to please an audience, although there are many theories. Shakespeare's solution was to have a character come on at the end of the play with an epilogue where everyone is asked to clap. Some people are more cynical about audiences.

The Austrian writer Thomas Bernhard was cynical and pessimistic about the value of audience applause, as he described in his poem " Le But": 107

people do not understand anything but will applaud to the death if they feel like applauding they applaud the most absurd things they would even applaud their own funerals they applaud all the blows they receive one hits them from the footlights and they applaud there is no greater perversity than the perversity of the theatre public [1]

Actors have to be extremely receptive and aware, ready to react to audiences that behave differently every night. Audiences are volatile, unpredictable, present – breathing the same air as the actors. They can be adversely affected by the weather, the traffic, or many other personal external conditions over which the theatre company has no control. There is always a sense of tension and excitement on both sides of the performance space, and anticipation on the part of the audience as they wonder if the evening they have sacrificed is going to live up to their expectations. When it does work, and the audience and performer connect across the dark divide, from stage to audience and vice versa, they become one, and both sides know it. It becomes a unique and unforgettable experience. When it really does work, the actors and the production team know that they have reached out to the unknown spectators, and in the suspended dramatic time of the performance have come to know them and affect them in a way that can only happen when the audience is given the gift of a live theatre performance.

This is the moment when all the analysis of the space; the preparation of the text; the background research; the translation of the vision into a colourful stage composition; the presentation of the actors in the direction of the production, come into focus – the interaction with the audience. The test for the scenographer is to see whether all the preparation has been in balance, and the spectators have understood the vision and the intention of the production. There are some very practical steps to be taken. If spectators cannot see, they cannot hear. So much depends on being able to see the actors' faces, and to follow the performer's eye line. When audiences can neither see nor hear, they lose their concentration, and quickly become restless. They cough, mutter, rustle their programmes, and ask each other what is being said. The acting area has to be planned from the beginning from the spectators' viewpoint (Figure 7.1). Three-dimensional computer programmes that can model the whole stage in plan and elevation with the

1   My translation from the French, Théâtre du Coin Programme.

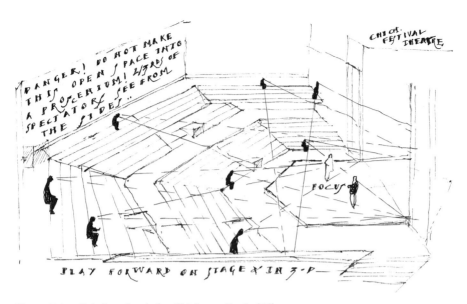

Figure 7.1   Sightline sketch for Chichester Festival Theatre

sightlines plotted in, have made this an easy exercise. However, when I work in three dimensions in a maquette, I still need to devise for myself a physical manifestion of the computer information. I build in a system of looking at the maquette from the spectators' point of view, which is hard because the human eye does not scale itself down to the normal measure of twenty-five times smaller than real life. I always make the first few rows of the audience in scale, using seated figures to mark the extreme seats. I then construct from thin wood or metal, a "sightline machine" – a geometric construction that represents the lines of sight from all the extreme seats in the auditorium, including the gallery and the balcony. I colour code them so I can identify which is which, and I can test out the ideas in the model by placing the "sightline machine" in front of the model, and looking at it from the correct distance. If, as sometimes happens, we decide that the space on the stage is too restricted for the action, we can then make a decision to convince the theatre management that some seats should not be sold. It is better to have fewer seats with good sightlines and an attentive audience, than to try to sell all the seats, and have some spectators who cannot see.

This care and respect for the spectator to receive only the best, was very much a signature of Caspar Neher's work with Bertolt Brecht, and the source of Brecht's admiration for his friend and colleague the painter and stage designer.

❖

I learned this at first hand when the Berliner Ensemble visited the Old Vic Theatre in London in 1965. I had been a fully fledged if embryonic theatre designer for five years. I volunteered to assist the company as a helper, and like many others stood in the street marvelling as two great pantechnicons parked outside the scene dock of the nineteenth-century theatre disgorged scenery for the plays, all miraculously packed into one huge lorry. Like an American gangster movie, another lorry was totally packed with technicians, costumed in blue boiler suits embroidered with the Berliner Ensemble logo, one colour for those who worked on Stage Left and a different colour for those who worked on Stage Right. We had never seen technological organisation on this scale in the theatre, and at the time it seemed the epitome of perfection, one that we should all strive towards. I was chosen by Hélène Weigel (Brecht's wife and the famous Mother Courage) to help hang the exhibition of drawings by the scenographer Karl von Appen, whose works, along with those of the very different Caspar Neher, have influenced my own artistic career. What I learned from this encounter was the careful and detailed process of preparation that is necessary to make everything perfect "*for the audience*" as Weigel kept telling me. Impatient to see the beautiful coloured drawings, I wanted to get them on the wall, vaguely thinking they could be moved about to make them straight when they were all in place. But this was not at all the Berliner Ensemble way. First the pictures had to be laid on the floor with the right spaces between them. Before anything further could happen, they had to be inspected by Weigel herself, for no one else could give the authority to proceed to the next stage. The next stage was called "The marking out of the Dot where the Nail would eventually go", and this involved myself as dot marker supervised by three administrators. The pencil dots were inspected, altered and approved, and the nails (quality approved) were allowed to be put in a third of a centimetre to await another inspection. The nails were eventually driven into the wall, and the great moment came – not for the pictures to be hung but to be raised from face down on the floor, to vertically leaning against the wall, awaiting a final inspection from Weigel who was, at the same time, rehearsing Volumnia in *Coriolanus* on stage. The wires on the pictures were checked and tightened, and, on the fourth day, were put in place. They were perfect and needed no alteration at all. I learned an important lesson. Preparation is all, and nothing is too much trouble to present perfection to the spectator, who need not know of the effort involved but who has to be given the best possible chance of seeing what must be shown. Later Weigel gave me a book of drawings by the Polish graphic artist Tadeusz Kulisiewicz recording her performance as Mother Courage on the Berliner tour of Poland. This book is my most treasured possession, and has inspired me to record and draw the actors in preparation and rehearsal. Weigel not only gave me the book, but seeing that I was young and eager to learn, she brought me the blouse she wore in *The Mother* and the jacket she wore as Mother Courage, and through this introduced me to the art of Caspar Neher who had died in 1962. She gave me the understanding that everything that is shown in the theatre must be correct from every point of view – that of the performers, and that of the spectators, that of the scenographer and that of the technicians – and that one must always ask questions about the smallest detail until everyone is satisfied. Here she was, playing Volumnia, an epic role, yet paying attention to the humblest artefact. Most important was to ask the question "What do we want the spectator to understand from this?" She gave me the blouse and asked me to feel the fabric, and told me that Neher had always rubbed material between his fingers in a sensual way. It was essential to love the material. She told me what a long time they had spent experimenting with the blouse because they wanted the audience to understand immediately its history that would not be spoken on stage. I later read this description that matches word for word what she said to me, and I never forgot: "It [the blouse] was to be blue, but blue like calico that has been to the wash a couple of hundred times. Had it once had a pattern? Was this still visible? Had it picked up a blue or grey dye? Palm [the Dyer] made tests and juggled the blouse through every conceivable stage. Luxury with unluxurious material. In the end it was the most beautiful blouse in theatrical history." Sometimes the simplest things are the most memorable – beautiful because they are true. As this short apprenticeship came to an end, Hélène Weigel advised me to remember that "creation is about making decisions, and making decisions is the reflection of a personal vision".

The conclusion of this philosophy is to make the spectators feel valued, and aware of the importance of every small detail in the composition that has been prepared with such love and care.

Scenographers tread a tightrope between being good collaborators, able to share and subscribe to other people's visions, yet at the same time remaining in control of their own creativity. Often this frustration focuses itself most forcefully on how a play should be done and presented to engage a contemporary audience. By and large, a literary minded, even visually aware, director is primarily interested in casting well and creating a good production. A scenographer, spatially aware, may well be wondering how a well cast and good production could be even further enhanced by the space it is played in, using the audience as a visual component in the design. One of the attractions of the unconventional theatre space is that it unites players and spectators in a joint adventure and exploration of the space. They appear willing to venture to see productions in the most faraway and unusual spaces, travelling to quarries, surburban swimming baths, aircraft hangars, lakes and islands for the event. The spectators and performers become part of the scenographic scheme in a fluid playing space without a fixed point of view as in a proscenium theatre. Spectators can find themselves at one moment in intimate physical proximity to the performers, and in the next quite far away. They have to accept that in this kind of theatre they will not necessarily see everything on the same level all the time. They quickly learn not to expect every detail of the story to be illustrated for them, nor for the stage to be filled with overwhelming evidence of a vast production budget, but they are caught by a sense of the event or the occasion, and the anticipation of a novel experience. This is not in any way better than, or preferable to, good theatre well presented on a proscenium stage, but it does pose a challenge for productions to match up to audiences' ever-changing expectations.

Whatever the form of theatre that is chosen as appropriate for the play, it should aid the spectators to concentrate on the text, especially if they have the chance to see a new or unfamiliar work. The form itself can become part of the dramatic structure, and this can sometimes provide alternative solutions to staging plays that have previously been designated as problems. Sometimes I enjoy speculating over projects, without the restrictions and anxieties of actual productions, to see if there are ways of rethinking these assumptions, particularly if it seems that there ought to be a much wider audience for the play. I like to explore, in the privacy of the studio, possibilities of uniting the audience and players in one space, and focusing the audience's eye on one event, only to surprise them by setting up another scene, unnoticed, that will carry the story on in perhaps unexpected ways. I am interested in how scenography becomes a visual narrator, and the scenographer the map-maker of the space, and how quickly audiences can learn "the rules of the game" and what is expected of them.

I reflected on this as a spectator watching the Brazilian Teatro da Vertigen present their production of *Apocalypse 1.11* in the Cuartel San Carlos in Caracas. It was a most extraordinary sight. Hundreds of spectators shouting, fighting and clamouring to get into the eighteenth-century San Carlos Prison – a fearsome building where formerly hundreds of prisoners fought to get out. This truly was the most ironic space I had ever been in. So ironic, for it required a coach ride to get there, and the act of paying to be admitted only made it more desirable to get in. Everyone craved the experience of temporary incarceration. Imported generators illuminated the building, which normally has no electricity, softening its hard, mean edges against the night sky, creating a seductive and romantic atmosphere

Figure 7.2   Performance drawing of *Apocalypse 1.11* in the Cuartel San Carlos, Caracas

to this house of horror. The privileged ticket holders were led past guards and dogs, into a courtyard, to watch a small girl sitting on a rooftop oblivious of the expectant crowd below. Slowly the fearsome entrance doors opened and we, the spectators, became part of the story as we were led into a space we would never normally see which had been artfully and skilfully prepared for us. As soon as we entered the space we were in the shared world of performer and spectator, participating in a game where we did not know the rules in advance but, by buying the ticket, had contracted to play.

It is a dangerous sport – physically and emotionally. We spectators are required to be active. There is no escape. It is impossible to lie back in red plush seats and, during interminable moments, daydream or sleep, waking up sometime later having missed much. In such confined spaces the performers are so physically close to us that we become part of the action observed by the other spectators. Our rights have been taken away, and we must do so as we are commanded.

This brings back into the theatre arena the concept of danger – the performer as a wild unpredictable being capable of physical and mental manipulation. We move through the space meekly and obediently, subjugated to the dominant will of our temporary masters. A route has been prepared for us and we quickly learn, as the prisoners did, the basic rules for survival. The performer is the boss and the first thing is to get out of the way if we have unwittingly placed ourselves where a performer needs to be. We make way for a group of naked performers running at speed through standing spectators – and miraculously it works (Figure 7.2). Pathways appear, spaces enlarge and reduce like drops of oil floating on water. The fluidity of the ever-changing space replaces the textual, literary or narrative development we are used to in the conventional divided theatre space. There is very little character or psychological development between characters, as this "event theatre" demands a full-volume, presentational type of performance. A different kind of temporality is introduced – one in which the past and present are brought together in a provocative and challenging way that is the actuality of the moment. There is no humour, and no relief. I thought of Bertolt Brecht's maxim "a theatre that can't be laughed in is a theatre to be laughed at"[2] and choked back a desire to laugh at the ridiculousness of the event.

But, like the old puppet theatres of Le Grand Guignol or Punch and Judy, these emblematic performances speak for the innermost minds of us silent, watchful prisoners, actualising and concretising our images of dreams and fantasies in a sensational manner. Sound and light become the scenographic mediums that animate and lead us through the spaces. Our visual and auditory senses are manipulated to focus on objects, real or constructed, that carry a metaphoric significance in the space beyond their reality. Often, the sudden illumination of an object contrasts violently in scale with the illuminated architecture and tells an entire story that words could not convey. Our attention is drawn by a rattling, scrabbling sound to a tiny, live, prisoner-rat confined in a cage, desperately trying to escape,

---

2   Bertolt Brecht, *Messingkauf Dialogues*, translated by John Willet, Methuen 1965.

at one end of a huge dramatic space – the disused prison refectory, its high vaulted ceiling heightened with light and shadow. Manipulation of scale within the architectural space provokes a confrontation between spectator and the non-verbal image that directly challenges our perception of where we are and what we understand by the image. Through this interplay of light and sound the secrets of the space are revealed.

The actors in their proximity and reality appear to be actually the people they are emblematically portraying, and their clothes versions of their own reality. These are no longer stage but space people. It is a long way from the custom of asking spectators to believe that when actors put on costumes they become other people who will pretend to love and suffer for a few hours, with the comfort of knowing they are just play-acting and will quickly return to normal. Even if this is not literally true, we spectators are easily convinced that it is. Just as in the cinema, the screen reality appears to be the actual reality. The actors defy us to turn away and lose eye contact as they present actual sexual acts in front of us with total conviction and daring. The illusion is only broken at the end when we realise we have been tricked. This is not the "here and now"; it will be done again tomorrow, and the day after, as the performance continues to be shaped and reshaped in response to different spaces. We realise that we have only played a game, and we have been deceived into believing this was reality. Our experience in prison, however, has made us all realise that the one thing no one can take away from us is our imagination, and if we had to suffer all this to realise it – well, the event was totally worth while and we survived the assault.

In this context, I have been experimenting for many years with the great Spanish classic *La Celestina*, wondering how it might be staged and its comedy and tragedy made more accessible to an English audience. *La Celestina* is thought of as a "large play", difficult and expensive to stage. It is a great Spanish classic normally included as part of a national theatre's repertoire, attracting all the attendant financial support. I want to release it from its stifling national treasure straitjacket, and create a fresh but truthful re-presentation that capitalises on its imagistic brilliance and visual allusions.

The story begins and ends in a walled garden which has been constructed for the young and beautiful Melibea by her over-protective father. In between there are many fast-moving scenes in different houses and parts of the city, many of which are "split" with simultaneous action happening both inside and outside. I have imagined finding a space,

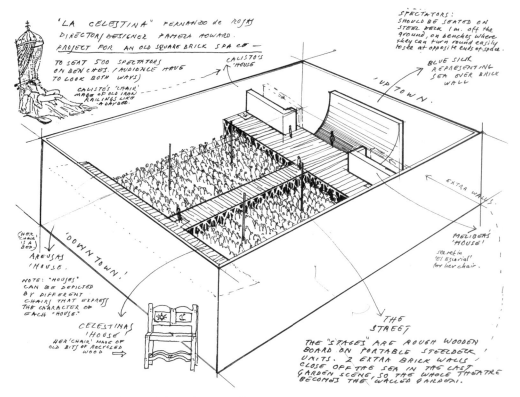

Figure 7.3   Sketch of the audience/performance space, *La Celestina*

perhaps a warehouse or old industrial building, which would be a brick or stone rectangle in which the spectators could feel that they too are incarcerated in the garden that becomes the visual envelope for the play. In order to facilitate the many moments where characters are running through the streets to one house of safety or another, there is a central planked walkway linking two raked wooden stages at either end. The constricted space is a metaphor for the totalitarian regime of Their Catholic Majesties Ferdinand and Isabella. The audience sits between the walkway and the stages, on benches placed on raised seating blocks enabling them to turn from end to end as the action moves (Figure 7.3). The actors are able to make journeys in many directions across the "streets". Four different house interiors are required, and these are suggested by specially made chairs, each one reflecting the character, class and status of its owner, and placed in the four corners of the walled garden. The character of the author,

116

Fernando de Rojas, also doubles as the father and has to be able to speak directly to the audience, and, by turning and walking a few steps, be in the next scene. The scenographic arrangement of the action within a strong architectural space gives form to the production, with the single purpose of enhancing the audience's experience of seeing, possibly for the very first time, this great, sad and comic play. Of course, as other collaborators join this ongoing research, it develops, and may well finally take another form altogether, but personal investment of time into scenographic research is never wasted and is essential to creative work.

Researching in this way, leading to small experimental workshops with players and spectators, is how the Venezuelan production of *Variaciones sobre un Concierto Barroco* began, created by the architect and scenographer Edwin Erminy. Architects are trained to consider the flow of people through a space, and placing, manipulating and moving audiences as part of the scenic invention. Spectators, unaware of their important role, are treated as essential to the story, and in this belief the stage space graphically unites giver and receiver. The text was adapted from the novella by the magic realist Cuban writer Alejo Carpentier, and is a journey play moving in time from 1704 to the present day, and from Latin America through Spain to Venice, where the story stops though does not end. It was decided from the beginning to explore working in a large empty space where the seating could be arranged and rearranged as appropriate. The playing space is defined by nothing more than twelve old wooden doors painted bright red, some laid flat on the floor on old pallets to become separate performing stages, and others attached vertically to the end scaffolding structures. The space had to have enough room for the actors to use the entire diagonal as the axis for the action of the play. Colour, a bright signal red, is used to unite the audience seating areas with the playing space by clothing all the seats in red "dresses" – elastic-sided covers specially made in a universal size to fit over chairs and seating blocks. In the empty theatre these 350 red chairs eerily resemble a silent audience of ladies in red flamenco dresses waiting for the bull-fight to begin. The doors are both exits and entrances. Great attention is given to how the audience arrives in the theatre. They are invited to enter and to play their part. The audience is first assembled at the front of the theatre, but, instead of coming in through the foyer, are led through a back door into rarely seen technical areas of the theatre and then into the auditorium. On the way, they pass through a corridor where they can glimpse the artifice of the theatre, through an installation constructed from discarded props and costumes, and bits of scenery from past operas dimly lit by builders' lamps. This has a half-finished and temporary look, but as the audience gets nearer to the entrance the installation becomes more specific. Rows of redundant red plush theatre seats with a gauze thrown over them and lit by a blue light from below support a tiny boat made out of scraps of old wood found on the workshop floor. The passing spectators immediately recognise it as an ocean. Mysterious singing is faintly heard as the audience approaches in single file and enters through a red door in a frame held open for them by an actress who welcomes each person individually exactly as if they were her personal guests. This is done in the local language, and the audience is surprised and enchanted by her efforts to speak correctly. The Hostess introduces her "guests" to each other at random taking care not to embarrass those who clearly just want to sit down with no participation. In the twenty minutes allowed for this "entrance of the audience" the sense of theatre as celebration is firmly established, and the audience is more than ready to play its part. No matter what gloomy predictions may have been made that spectators do not want to be "involved", in the many countries visited this device has never been a problem, and has always set the key to telling a strong, fast-moving story with political and cultural themes. Across the diagonal playing space, in the centre, is another free-standing red door frame with a door made of little windowpanes with no glass that opens onto an small empty playing space. The players, through their actions, convince the audience that door opening indicates an "interior" or an "exterior" by the direction they walk through. All the workings of the show – pulleys, ropes, curtains, technicians and stage management – are visible to the audience, who are intrigued by the simple magic performed before their eyes. The final part of *Concierto Barroco* has to convey a dress rehearsal of Vivaldi's opera *Montezuma* in the opera house in Venice in 1707. Two principal actors sit in the audience as spectators in a theatre within a theatre and they make loud comments to each other about the opera across the auditorium, which is both the actual warehouse and the imagined baroque theatre space. They ridicule the ludicrous plot and its staging. Through the actors' eyes and vocal contact the audience really believe in the reality of the opera house. Throughout *Concierto Barroco* the story is constantly interrupted by two contemporary cooks who act as narrators, in the form of presenters of a TV cookery programme. However, their TV kitchen is improvised and imaginary, for in another part of the playing space there is a real cook cooking real food, creating the enticing smells of a traditional dish of black beans and white rice that the theatre guests will be offered by the actors at the end of the performance. Finally, the hostess bids farewell and goodnight to everyone as they exit through another free-standing red door frame into the reality of the night.

This has been variously played in an unloved and unused space in the workshop basement of the national theatre of Caracas; on the planked-over auditorium and stage of a baroque theatre with its gold-tiered boxes and balconies; in the cloister of a convent; and in a large empty warehouse in London. The production can expand or contract to suit the chosen space, and needs, for economic reasons, to play to an audience of 350 people each night. Whatever the space, the criteria are the same – the theatre is a home, and the spectators are the guests.

The public are consumer-conscious and sophisticated. For some, it is deeply engaging to be a spectator watching other people pretending to be other people. Others are irritated by a live actor talking to them. Live performance demands a direct connection between giver and receiver, and impinges upon personal privacy. It is the opposite from the one-to-one relationship from a seat to a screen. They expect modern technology to be at their service, so that they can participate without effort. They look for magic, enchantment, transformation, and scenic effects that ravish the eye

Figure 7.4   Drawing for *The Cherry Orchard*

Figure 7.5   Drawing for *The Cherry Orchard*

and soothe the spirit. What they also look for is an opportunity to be transported from their own lives into another reality for a short time. This can be achieved by elaborate or simple means. It is here that the scenographer plays a major role. Either vast amounts of money can be spent imitating reality, using stage effects and machinery that become the stars of the show, or the scenographer can use invention and illusions of scale that provide a feast of delights for the audience.

This invites players and spectators to participate in theatre as celebration, with music, food and storytelling, and uses the spectators as the active scenographic ingredient. For a short time, the spectators agree to allow themselves to rediscover the simple naïvety of play and illusion. There is a thrill shared by performers and spectators on meeting each other in close proximity in the theatre space, and knowing that for a few hours the power of the production will transport everyone away from the everyday into a land of the imagination. The conviction of the performers can make the spectators see beauty and richness where there are only rags. Full-scale productions can be created out of nothing, and when presented with total belief create a rich theatre out of little means, grander than the most grand spectacle, and thrill audiences with their simple invention. In Brecht's poem "The Masters Buy Cheap" he describes the art of scenography:

> The decors and costumes of the great Neher
> Are made of cheap material
> Out of wood, rags and colour
> He makes the Basque fisherman's hovel
> And imperial Rome.

AFTERWORD

"What is Scenography?"
or "What's in a Name."[1]

A few years ago, I was invited to work with a young and gifted director to design Shakespeare's *King Henry IV Parts I and II* that would be presented together as one marathon performance. These two "state of the nation" plays depict in twenty-nine swiftly moving scenes the debt-ridden English, bankrupted by war expenditure, the death of the old King Henry IV, and the rise of the young Prince Hal, who through his own political and moral awakening becomes England's new hope – King Henry V.

Occasionally art and life collide, and the time seemed just right to do these plays. Great Britain was entering a moment of political change, emerging from an eighteen-year Conservative rule in favour of a younger, eager group of politicians calling themselves New Labour. There was a new freedom in the air, and we fantasised that the restrictive practices, class distinctions, negativity and cultural philistinism of the past years would change. Perhaps there would be a new and more flexible attitude towards race, gender, age, and maybe the traditional hierarchies that replicate themselves in repeated behaviour patterns from generation to generation would finally change.

Drama has the power to show the actuality of the present day, through the metaphor of history, and we were intoxicated by the relevance of these old history plays. The director, assistant director, and myself agreed to approach the task with no preconceived ideas – to start from an equal empty slate. We decided to spend three days away, simply reading and understanding the text, and booked into a typically English bed and

1   Keynote address to the USITT given by the author on 21 March 2001, Long Beach, California.

breakfast, appropriately furnished with reproduction Elizabethan furniture and a collection of china cats.

In this bucolic rolling countryside we read out loud to each other, taking any part in turn and asking each other just what had been said by who and to whom. As we were reading, I began making visual notes, not designs, to clarify who had entered the scene, and when, and how the dramatic power shifts from one group of characters to another. Our textual misreadings became clear through the drawings that concretised the words. I drew the moment we had just read, placing figures in an empty and as yet unknown space. The drawings became the storyboard. Objects began to suggest themselves to make the story clearer and more truthful – a chair, a tree, a candle, a bed. We worked quickly and intensely, covering the twenty-nine scenes in these three days. At the end of this retreat, we went our own ways, full of ideas and thoughts to reflect upon, sure that we now knew the difference between Warwick, Worcester and Westmoreland.

Back in my studio I laid out the drawn notations in sequence on my drawing table. The image evoked by the king's words that open the play was floating before my eyes: "No more the thirsty entrance of this soil/Shall daub her lips with her own children's blood . . ." I thought of the red earth of the Shropshire hills, ancient battles, and the network of canals that like veins and arteries are deep, red incisions that cross that countryside. The blood of the children would be invisible against the earth. I started to add strong, simple blocks of colour and immediately, as I grouped the figures against this red earth, the colours reminded me of the world of the fourteenth-century painter Massacio, that had been the subject of a former collaboration in London with the Bread and Puppet Theatre of the USA.

We had created a production based on Masaccio's frescoes which can be seen in the Brancacci chapel in Florence. He was the first social realist painter, and portrayed young Italian men defiantly arguing with officials, tax collectors, and elder citizens. Their frustration at their repression is evident from the posture and facial expressions that we had captured in the exaggerated masks and figures we had designed, made and performed with. This visual cross-referencing was the key to unlocking our own interpretation of these plays.

In *King Henry IV Part II* Shakespeare reflects through Warwick: "There is a history in all men's lives." I began to study in depth the characters and invent their histories, to get to know them as people. I became more and more fluent at describing the space scenographically, working from the actor outwards. Together, the director and myself (for the work was united and indivisible) created over fifty drawings, charting like air traffic controllers the expansion and contraction of the scenes, through the movement of actors that made the space speak.

In this way, the stage scenario was written, and all was in harmony. Then at a pre-production meeting, I said quite idly and casually "Oh, by the way, this time credit me in the programming as scenographer, not as 'designer' because scenographer describes more precisely the way I work." There was a stunned silence. Everyone looked uncomfortably at each other. I was surprised. Was this a contentious issue? I wondered what the problem was. "What would happen," said the general manager, "if everyone wanted to be called a scenographer? – we just would not be able to cope." "I am sure there won't be enough room on the programme," said the marketing manager, "and we can't afford any more pages – our budget is stretched as it is." The technical director thought it sounded as though a scenographer might be working too much with the director, and would not do the technical drawings properly. My friend and colleague the director was a bit abashed and embarrassed, feeling caught in a trap. He thought scenographer sounded un-English, perhaps rather French or German, and implied a "*folie de grandeur*". And then, one person, the Director of Education, asked: "But what is scenography?" I suddenly realised how important a name is.

Scenography describes a holistic approach to making theatre from the visual perspective. It derives from the Greek *sceno-grafika*, and translated in common understanding as "the writing of the stage space – *l'écriture scènique*". It is an international theatre word. It is not stenography, or sexography, or a spelling mistake. As the word is becoming more and more familiar in countries where it has not been in common use, so it becomes locally interpreted. At the same time, scenography and scenographers are taking a different path from theatre designers (often now mistaken for those who design theatres) and are sometimes crossing the demarcation lines between direction and design, becoming joint creators of the *mise en scène*.

The acceptance of the word "scenography, or scenographer" is no more than an attitude of mind. It begins by including it on the programme and printed material so that it becomes a normal and accurate description of an activity. Out of sight is always out of mind.

To be called a scenographer means more than decorating a background for actors to perform in front of. It demands parity between creators, who each have individual roles, responsibilities and talents. The prerequisite for going forward in this new century of theatre-making starts with all the different disciplines involved in creating a production having a better understanding of each other's work processes and achievements. I once heard a well-known technical director muttering to himself as he walked down a corridor, "If it wasn't for the actors, and the director, and the designers, I could get this show on the road with no trouble at all . . ." Those days are surely gone.

The scenographer also has to work harder to understand the needs of the performers, who are, in the end, the primary visual element one has to work with. What the performers wear is both a signifier of the plot, or story, and an extension of the stage picture. The actors are the scenography, and therefore to separate "sets" from "costumes" is, in scenographic terms, a contradiction. However, in order for the scenographer to be part of the *mise en scène* there has to be a structure that enables them to be in rehearsals as a partner to the director, so that the literary mind and the visual mind can work together. The scenographer needs to be part of the process, and to understand the actors' performances and how to sculpt them in the space. Actors are the carriers of the story, and are brave, tender and vulnerable and often need help to see themselves as three-dimensional beings in the graphic space. Through drawings and maquettes they can be reminded of the scene as viewed by the spectators. Yet, however well explained the maquette is at "show and tell" sessions at the beginning of rehearsals – how quickly it is forgotten. How many times have we seen a carefully marked-out stage plan on the rehearsal floor, with actors being directed to walk through walls, ignoring doorways, and putting chairs where there are stairs. The fact is that the rehearsal process is fluid and ever changing, but the system usually demands advance decision and precision. So often, by the time the production moves from the rehearsal room to the technical fit up on the stage, the two concepts no longer match, and enormous "damage limitation" exercises have to be put in place in order to reach what is often no more than a compromise.

The visible emergence of the scenographer is not some wilful whim dreamt up by frustrated theatre designers who feel they have not been properly recognised, or who are tired of being treated in ignoble and humiliating ways by their colleagues. The rise of the scenographer as someone who is willing to take on extra responsibilities in the creation of a production is born out of a very real concern for the state of the art, and the economic and political climate we live and work in.

126   In every country the same sad story is to be heard. Lack of money,

inadequate funding, embattled theatre-makers, marginalised existences, subsidies used to maintain buildings, artists accepting the role of unnamed sponsors by working for nothing, or the equivalent of poverty pay, in order just to make their work. The irony is that there is money available to do almost anything to do with theatre other than create the work. Conferences, exhibitions, international meetings, creation of databases and job surveys abound. Sourcing funding, and completing application forms, and report forms, has become the all-consuming activity. It is even possible to get funding to go on courses to learn how to apply for funding. Soon it will be time to have a Prague Quadrennial exhibition based on all the productions that did not happen over the past four years. Nearly every meeting, lecture or discussion about theatre ends up not talking about the art but anguishing about the all too evident lack of money, and the apparent limited understanding of the "philistines" who hold the purse strings in whatever government happens to be in power.

The making of theatre, sometimes better, sometimes worse, largely replicates existing custom and practice. Theatre-making large or small is in a chronic state of lurching from one crisis to another, in a negative equity, with practitioners feeling that their voices are seldom heard and never listened to, while the modern-day gods – Money, Marketing, and Management – aim not to spend inadequate budgets.

The scenographer, looking at this situation, and being the most visible spender of the money, can either feel completely restricted or, if given the opportunity, become completely liberated. This suggests rethinking the conventional role that defines design as an applied art seeking to assert a "visual individuality" to rival the director's "concept" and the actor's "performance". The aim of the scenographer should be to rediscover how to make theatre that uses the resources available to the best effect both artistically and economically, and they need to be empowered to do this.

Normally the production is decided by the Director, and then cast into the appropriate roles. The reasons for choosing to do a particular production are frequently incomprehensible. Too often a huge production is conceived without the means to realise it. A budget is drawn up that relates to the potential income, but not to the needs or the demands of the work. The designer therefore becomes a damage limitator, and considers it part of the job to find solutions to impossible problems.

Theatre-makers are starting to realise that this continual state of crisis is not a crisis at all, but a state of being, and many – particularly scenographers, visual artists of the theatre – feel empowered to take matters into their own hands. The example of the crossovers in painting and performance art has encouraged visual artists to instigate new work, strengthening that fragile vessel called theatre. It is not beyond the bounds of possibility to see scenographers taking a more visible role in programme and policy planning, and proposing directors they find interesting and want to work with. It is a small but significant shift of emphasis.

To participate in change, to try to improve the working conditions and therefore the quality of the work, demands putting one's own house in order first. Can we, scenographers, honestly say that we do not collude with the very structures that inhibit our activity, using it as an excuse for not being able to achieve something – "I can't be as creative as I would wish, because the costume shop wants all the designs in three months before the production is cast" – for example. When we can no longer go out and buy ready made food will we still remember how to make delicious homemade food at half the cost? Any woman who has run a home, brought up children and done a full-time job knows both how to produce quality goods on a budget and how to adapt to circumstance without compromising strongly held beliefs. Scenographers know how to invent, create and manipulate – be counsellors, politicians, leaders, workers, artists, and still be creative cooks. The combination of women and scenographers is alchemy.

I have not invented scenography. It is not a new religion or even a new idea. It's just that I have begun using and speaking the name, and others do it too. And to everyone's surprise the world does not come to an end – a third world war does not start. Life appears to go on much as before. But there is a difference. Scenographers, whether their main interest is with light, actors, space, or scenery, have become more visible and do have a new voice. They are heard, and people do use the word, openly and with less and less hesitation. We have come out – become visible, and with that have actively accepted the responsibilities for change that go with a new description. We are now able to say, just as people before have identified themselves with a group, "I am a scenographer." International boundaries are disappearing, while individual groups develop clearer identities. If theatre mirrors life, then the strict demarcations between theatre disciplines, architecture, light, direction, writing, are also merging, into a different kind of creation in which the scenographer is now a major player.

The principles of scenography are the principles of Art. The seventeenth-century painter Jean-Siméon Chardin challenged the status quo of the French Academy to reassert his belief in Art as the communicator. He rejected the large, purely narrative picture in favour of focusing the viewer's attention to seeing the familiar anew – selected for them by the artist's eye. A teacup, a jar of apricots, a silver spoon – he makes the ordinary appear extraordinary. Objects and figures become, as in theatre, emblematic, the carriers of the myth, heightened by darkness and light, and adding value to the empty space. All the elements of scenography are contained in the geometric spaces placed within a conventional frame. Chardin is a teacher for theatre artists, for, as the painter Mark Rothko said 250 years later: "In simplifying the present, he re-invents the future." That is scenography.

POSTSCRIPT

What is scenography?
Scenography is the seamless synthesis of space, text, research, art, actors, directors and spectators that contributes to an original creation.

INDEX

Note: references to illustrations are in *italics*.

131